MONGOLIA

*The natural grandeur of
Mongolia casts a spell on the
beholder.*

Following page 4: *A bridge
with the Gobi Desert in the
distance.*

MONGOLIA

The Land of Blue Skies

GAURI SHANKAR GUPTA

Photographs by
Thomas L. Kelly

Lustre Press
Roli Books

ISBN: 978-81-7436-454-8

© Roli & Janssen BV 2007
This edition published in arrangement with
Roli & Janssen BV, The Netherlands
M-75 Greater Kailash II (Market),
New Delhi 110 048, India
Ph: ++91-11-29212782, 29210886;
Fax: ++91-11-29217185
E-mail: roli@vsnl.com; Website: rolibooks.com

Editor: Padma Pegu
Design: Nitisha Mehta
Layout: Naresh L Mondal
Production: Naresh Nigam, Kumar Raman

Printed and bound in Singapore

ACKNOWLEDGEMENTS

The rugged, starkly picturesque landscape of Mongolia, its nomadic lifestyle, its immensely rich cultural heritage, and its civilisational legacy have always fascinated me. I had a first glimpse of this beautiful land and its hospitable people in 1993, during a short visit to Ulaanbaatar. My fascination became more and more intense, particularly from June 2003, when I reached there on assignment as ambassador of India to Mongolia. I was, therefore, keen to write about this beautiful land of blue skies and its people. My daughter Deepika, who has been inspiring me to write, further fortified my resolve.

About the same time, an opportunity presented itself – Roli Books was looking for somebody to author a book on Mongolia. During her visit to India Ms Nadine Kriesberger, a French national who was working in Mongolia as adviser to Dr S. Oyun, member of parliament, suggested my name to Amit Agarwal of Roli Books. Soon thereafter, I received an email from Amit offering me the assignment. Although I was then extremely busy with my official duties, I accepted the offer as it was dear to my heart.

Since time was short, I immediately started collecting facts and figures and started preparing a chapter-by-chapter manuscript. My secretary P. Anand did a wonderful job in deciphering the manuscript and putting it into electronic version during his spare time and weekends. Ms Padma Pegu did a highly professional job in editing the text and putting it more coherently and in reader-friendly manner. Of course, the heart and soul of this publication comes from the professional photographs provided by Thomas Kelly. These photographs were taken by him during his extensive travels around the country.

I am, therefore, indebted to Nadine, Amit, Anand, Padma and Thomas for their valuable support in completion of this project. It is a matter of immense pleasure for me that the project has been realised during the 800th anniversary of Mongolia's statehood.

Since my daughter Deepika and son Kartikaya have been persistently inspiring me to write, I dedicate this book to them.

Gauri Shankar Gupta

Gandan monastery in Ulaanbaatar, Mongolia.

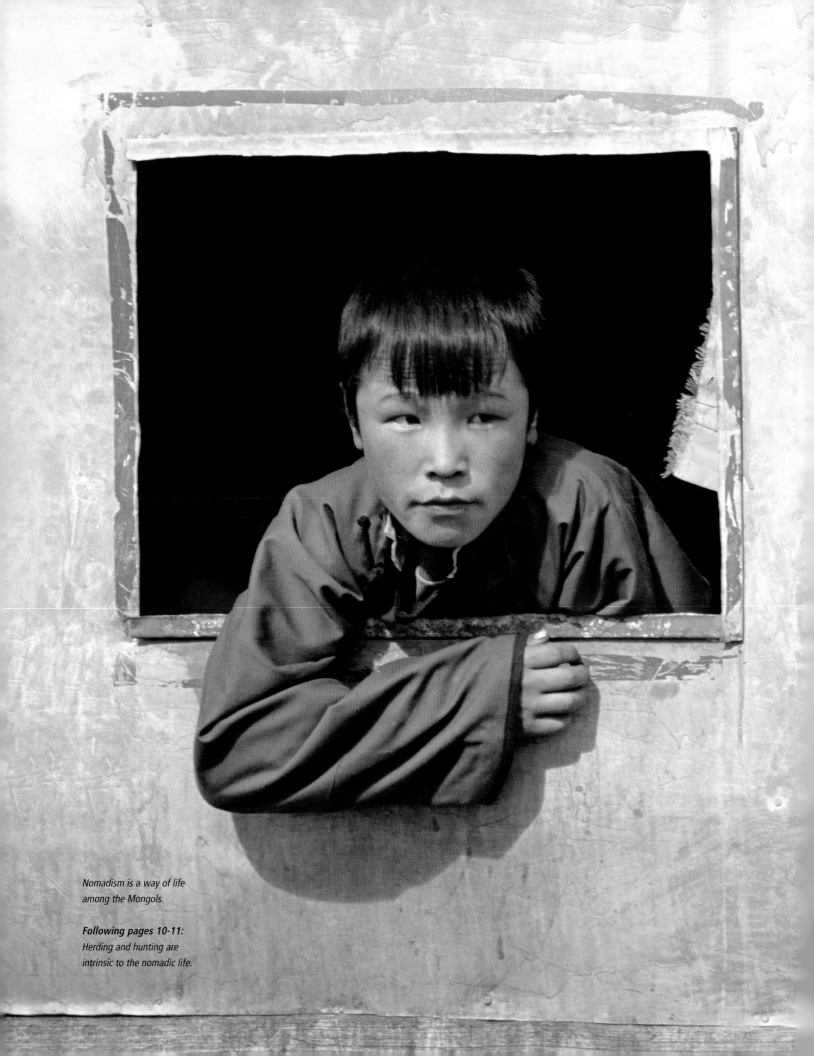

Nomadism is a way of life among the Mongols.

Following pages 10-11:
Herding and hunting are intrinsic to the nomadic life.

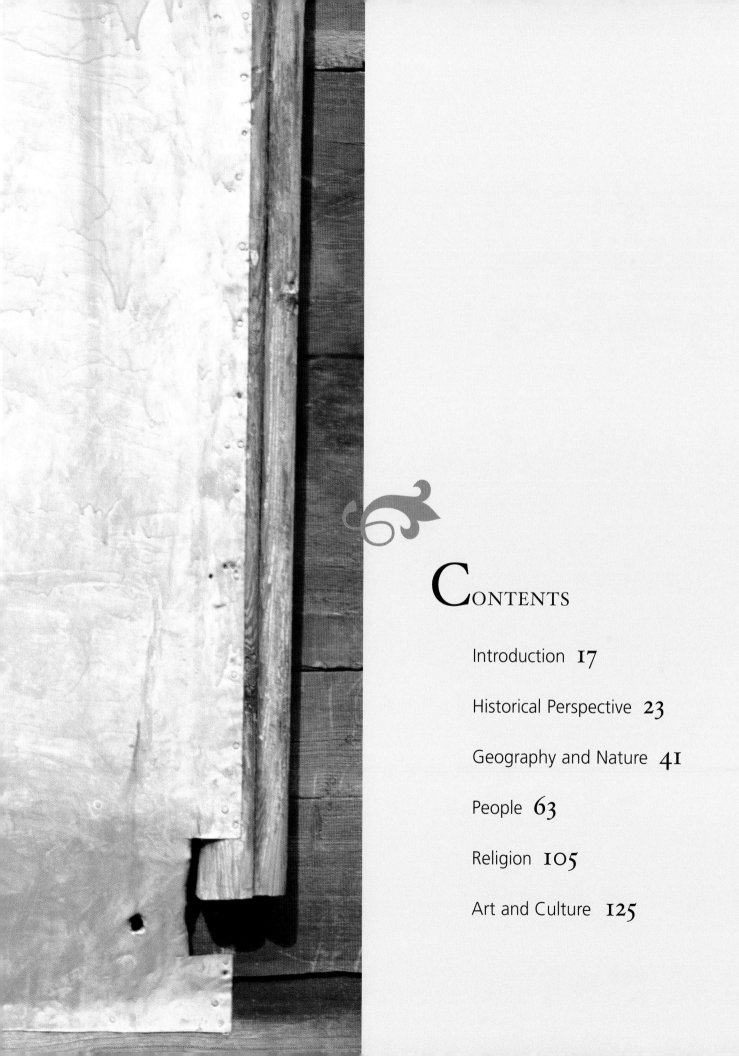

Contents

N

RUSSIA

Huvsgul
Lake

Uvs
Lake

Ulaangom

Hatgal

Oligii

Hyargas
Lake

Far
Northern
Region

Moron

Egiyn R

Bulgan

Dund-us

Ider R

Orhon R

Altai
Mountains
Region

Har Us
Lake

Uliastay

Bulgan

Tsetserleg

Altai

Arvaikheer

Bayankhongor

M O N G O

MONGOLIA

The Land of Blue Skies

Baikal Lake

CHINA

Salanga R

Onon R

Darkham

Kerulan R

ULAANBAATAR

Tuul R

Ondorhaan

Nomadic Central Steppes

Mandaigovi

L I A

Buyant-Uhaa

Dalandzadgad

Gobi Desert Region

CHINA

A rider on horseback crosses the Arkhangai river, near Tsetserleg, in central Mongolia. Many Mongolians learn to ride horses very early on in life and are known to be expert riders.

INTRODUCTION

Located in the heart of Asia, between Russia and China, Mongolia is a cradle of nomadic civilisation. Teeming with galloping horses, freely roaming yaks, slow-moving two-hump camels, rare species of wild animals and birds, and infinite horizons with a canopy of vast blue sky, the land is simply exotic. Sustained by a population of 27 million herds, about 40 per cent Mongolians still live the nomadic way of life. They install their portable dwelling called *ger* in the middle of nowhere and live like royalty amidst nature, in complete harmony with their animals. The vast territory of 1.56 million square kilometres is adorned by snow-covered mountains, glaciers, beautiful lakes, vast steppes, and the super-arid Gobi Desert. Known as 'the land of blue skies', Mongolia has over 300 clear sunny days in a year. Nevertheless, the climate is almost extreme, with temperatures ranging between -59°C and +50°C.

Harmonious existence of various religions was a great positive contribution of the Mongols, the roots of which rest in Shamanism. Shamanism was the earliest religion prevalent among the Mongolian nomads.

Inside their teepee Tsaatan reindeer nomads make tea and offer their reindeer chunks of salt.

Conspicuous as it remains by its relative obscurity and low-key profile, the country has a rich legacy of civilisation going back to the 3rd century BC – to the Hun Empire. In the 12th and 13th centuries, the legendary Chinggis Khan – the great son of Mongolia – ruled the largest-ever land empire on earth and prepared the foundation for the famous Yuan dynasty, established by his grandson Kubilai Khan.

Even with a sparse population of about 2.6 million people, the Mongols have distinguished themselves in almost every walk of life. The land has produced master painters and sculptors, writers and poets, sturdy sportsmen and warriors, and skilled dancers and musicians. Hardened by the harsh climatic conditions, people are tough and intelligent with a very strong survival instinct. Given such compelling qualities, it is not surprising that Mongolia has survived as an independent nation despite the frequent invasions on its sovereignty. For these very reasons, Mongolians often say that those who constructed the Great Wall must be great, but those who forced them to construct it, must be greater! Today, Mongolia is a nation that boasts a vibrant democracy, a free media, high rate of literacy, and a rich cultural and artistic heritage.

Shamanist and Tibetan Buddhist traditions run deep in the blood of Mongolian people. These traditions have left an indelible mark on the religious, spiritual and artistic legacy of the Mongolian civilisation. Shamanist traditions are woven in nature worshipping and ecological preservation, while Buddhist traditions lay down the foundation for peaceful coexistence. The

monasteries and temples provide a perfect abode for meditation and enlightenment. Despite the religious purge of the 1930s and 40s, these traditions continue to be an inseparable part of Mongolian culture and folklore. Today, Mongolians are nurturing their roots by reconstructing monasteries and religious literature and art, as also by restoring the faith of their children. As part of this resurrection, Chinggis Khan has emerged as their national hero. His name reverberates in everything Mongolian, from airport to city hubs to *ger* camps to vodka and beer.

While the Mongolian countryside remains pristine and pure, the cities have begun to be touched by modernisation and globalisation. Free market economy has engendered a new hunger for money and luxury. At the same time, while economic activities are rapidly expanding, the gulf between the rich and the poor – and between the city dwellers and the nomads – is also widening. Factors like increasing migration to cities, reckless exploitation of mineral resources, and growing tourism are posing new dangers to the nomadic way of life as well as to the so-long-unsullied environment. Yet, these are the realities of modern life in a globalised world which cannot be suppressed or kept away. Perhaps this new experience must be lived in order to realise the value of the old. In course of time, they will find their own balance and blend. The old and the new must coexist.

Nevertheless, despite the imprint of globalisation, Mongolia is still one of the most fascinating destinations on this planet. Its rich cultural heritage, landscapes awash with raw

Hardened by the harsh climatic conditions, the Mongolian nomad has developed a strong survival instinct.

Horses have provided reliable transportation for Mongolians for thousands of years. Mongol cowboy lassoing horses.

natural beauty, and strong traditions of hospitality are quite without parallel. The Mongolian countryside provides an experience that is splendid and unforgettable. A journey to this land of infinite horizons and blue skies is a journey of a lifetime. This is a journey into the wild, to touch and feel the unexplored, and to experience the unexpected. This is a unique adventure – for some a leap in darkness, for others a goldmine. For those who are unmindful of the comforts of modern life, a journey in the wilderness of Mongolia's virgin lands is a journey closer to heaven.

Historical

PERSPECTIVE

A cradle of nomadic civilisation, Mongolia occupies a pivotal place in Central Asia. Mongolians were among those who crossed the narrow Bering Strait and established the first human settlements in the American continent. The Mongols also have the distinction of ruling the largest-ever land empire on earth. Although archaeological finds in Orkhon River valley, Selenge, Tula and elsewhere have confirmed that the present-day territory of Mongolia was once inhabited by prehistoric settlers, the first recorded appearance of nomads is traced back to the 4th – 3rd centuries BC. Successive nomadic societies and their cultures were primarily based on domestication of animals and migratory and tribal lifestyle. The nomadic people in the steppes north of Gobi were known for their bravery and feared by the sedentary Chinese, who inhabited the south of Gobi. Frequent invasions by nomads for control of resources and territory forced the Chinese to build a 2,300-kilometre-long Great Wall along their northern border. Chinese writings of those times described the nomads as 'barbarians living in the cold wilderness of the far north and impossible to rule as subjects'. They have also been called Hu, or 'primitive tribes' – savage in temper and belligerent.

Facing page:
The war memorial overlooking the capital city of Ulaanbaatar honours soldiers who died in battle, particularly in World War II.

Gilded silver crown with tall wings.

✒ EARLY PERIOD

In 209 BC the Huns, descendants of those ancient nomadic tribes, established the first state in Central Asia. These fierce tribal people controlled a vast territory – from Gobi Desert in the south to Lake Baikal in the north, and from Khingan mountains in the east to Erchis River in the west. The roots of the ethnic culture of modern Mongolia can be traced back to the Huns. The nomadic culture of these people earned the Hun Empire the epithet 'state on horseback'. The hundred and fifty years of Hun Empire not only united the nomadic tribes in the steppes, but also helped promote art, music, astronomy and astrology. It is believed that the 12-month lunar calendar was introduced during this period. The capital of the Hun Empire was located in the present-day Orkhon valley near Karakorum. Unfortunately, the mighty empire did not last long and collapsed following a fierce internal struggle during 55–53 BC. Once again, the nomads scattered all over the steppes and got divided into small tribal states.

The Juan-juan, Turkic, Uighur, Kirgiz and Khitan empires followed in succession. The Juan-juan state reached its zenith under Shelun, who in AD 402 assumed the title of Khagan. Although the lifestyle during the Juan-juan period was primarily nomadic, considerable advances were made in mathematics and astronomy. Several languages as well as a script existed during this period. In AD 555 the Juan-juan Khanate was defeated by the Altai Turks and thereafter, for almost five centuries, the Turks, Uighurs and Kirgiz people dominated the region. The bulk of the Juan-juan population became part of the Turkic Khanate. Archaeological finds clearly indicate a well-developed civilisation during this period.

Petroglyphs found on a rock in the Bayantsagaan valley in Mongolia.

The Turkic Khanate was replaced by the Uighurs, who were at their peak between AD 745 and AD 759 – during the rule of Moyunchur Khan. The capital of Uighur Empire, Khar Balgas, was situated on the left bank of Orkhon River. Construction of towns and fortresses, and introduction of handicrafts and jewellery are attributed to the Uighurs. A large number of gold, silver and bronze artefacts of the period have been found during archaeological excavations. The ruins of Khar Balgas are a vivid testimony to the advanced civilisation of that time. Even though nomadic culture was still predominant, there is evidence of agriculture and settled existence during this period. Writing was well-developed. A large number of inscriptions on rocks, barks, leather and cloth have been found. Some of the archaeological finds from this period have recently been housed in the Museum of Mongolian History in Ulaanbaatar. Although most people at the time were still Shamanists, many others were professing Buddhism. There were some followers of Nestorian Christianity, too.

A dragon carved in stone in the sparse ruins of Khar Balgas, the capital of Uighur Khanate in the 8th century.

At the end of the 8th century, the power of the Uighurs was on a steady decline. Internecine wars gave way to outside attacks. In AD 840, the Uighurs succumbed to attacks by the Yenisei Kirgiz. A new Kirgiz Khanate consisting of Turkish, Mongol and Kirgiz tribes was constituted. However, they did not last long and the Kirgiz were driven out by a Mongol tribe, the Khitans. From the 6th to 8th centuries, the Khitans had incessantly resisted the domination of the Turkic, the Uighurs and the Kirgiz. Over those years, they gained considerable strength and established the Khitan Empire in the mid-10th century. This was a feudal state with hereditary monarchy. The Khitan Empire included the central and southern parts of Mongolia and the north-eastern part of China. Archaeological excavations have confirmed that the Khitans were well-versed in town planning, metal smelting, and art and craft. They were primarily Shamanists, but after the formation of Liao dynasty (907–1125) the feudal upper class started professing Buddhism. Internal and external conflicts marked the short history of the Khitan Empire. Inter-tribal wars never allowed the Khitans to consolidate power to build a strong state structure. The empire disintegrated in the first half of the 12th century.

The prolonged domination of Mongolian territory by the Turkic people had forced several Mongolian tribes to move to the eastern and north-eastern parts of the country, forming small, separate khanates. During this phase, Mongolians had quite lost the fire so conspicuous during the Hun and Juan-juan rules. This period of regression led, on the one hand, to fresh thinking on Mongol nationalism among the tribes, and, on the other, to inter-tribal strife for supremacy. Efforts were made to revive tribal relations and create a federation. The largest Mongolian tribes at the time were Hamag, Hereid, Merged, Naiman and Tartars. The feudal aristocracy in these tribes wanted a strong state structure to support their status and power. In time, communal access to land and pastures gave way to private ownership by feudal lords. This development led to the division of society between the feudal lords and the herdsmen.

Ordinary nomadic people lost their social and economic freedom, and started working as herdsmen, servants, bodyguards, and so on. Thus, at the beginning of the 12th century each of the major Mongolian tribes had evolved a similar structure, and they were competing for power against each other. Under such conditions of feudal division and internecine wars, the *huree*, or ring-shaped disposition of towns, was widely used for defence against surprise attacks. Each *huree* normally consisted of 1,000 *gers* or *yurts*, with the leader's *ger* in the centre.

RISE OF TEMUJIN

By the beginning of the 11th century, Hamag Mongols had emerged as the leading clan of a loose federation. They inhabited the basins of three rivers – Orkhon, Herlen and Tuul. In the early 12th century, the Hamag *ulus* (state/khanate) was ruled by Kabul Khan. His grandson Yesugei-baatar ruled over the Taichuul, the largest of the Hamag Mongol tribes.

Temujin, the future Chinggis Khan, was born into Yesugei-baatar's family in Deluun Boldog – in the upper reaches of Onon River – in 1162. At the time of his birth he was reported to have manifested 'fire in his eyes and light in his face', and was, therefore, regarded as destined by the heavens for fame. In 1170, Yesugei-baatar was poisoned by the hostile Tartars and his *ulus* disintegrated thereafter. After his father's death, Temujin's mother Oelun lived in poverty and hardship. Battered by these struggles, Temujin became sharp, shrewd and brave. There are several anecdotes about his childhood in the manuscript *Secret History of the Mongols*.

According to the *Secret History*, relations between Temujin and his half brother Begter were not amiable. On one occasion, after a quarrel over a hunt, Temujin with his younger brother Kasar killed Begter in cold blood. Although this appears to be an act of cowardice, it indicates that Temujin could be ruthless to defend his leadership. Another episode took place when Temujin with another of his half brothers, Belgutei, was on a hunting trip. Thieves took away eight of his nine horses. While looking for the thieves, he met a handsome young man called Boorchu. Boorchu accompanied Temujin and helped him in recovering his horses from the thieves. Boorchu later on became the most trusted general of Temujin.

Above:
Chinggis Khan,
the national hero
of Mongolia.

Right: Seal of
the indomitable
Chinggis empire.

Temujin married Borte, daughter of the Hongirad tribal chief Dei Setsen, and started fighting for power over other tribes. Guided by his shrewd intellect and ambitions, he embarked on a political journey. He entered into an alliance with Tooril Khan (also known as Wang Khan), chief of the Hereid tribe – the second most influential tribe after the Hamags.

In 1184 the Merged tribe, which was at loggerheads with the Hamags, attacked Temujin's camp and kidnapped his mother. Temujin was able to bring back his mother, but his wife Borte was taken prisoner by the Mergeds. Temujin – who by then had mastered not only the art of political alliances, but also that of the battlefield – crushed the Mergeds with the help of Wang Khan and Prince Jamuha of the Jadran tribe, and brought his wife back. However, when Borte returned she was pregnant. Although the paternity was never properly established, Borte's first child Jochi carried the blemish of possible illegitimacy. He was therefore never considered equal by his younger brothers and not accepted as a true heir of Chinggis Khan.

Chinggis Khan married Borte, daughter of the Hongirad tribal chief Dei Setsen.

Temujin's victory over the Mergeds gave him considerable power, recognition and confidence. However, the Temujin-Jamuha alliance did not last long as both were competing for leadership of the Hamag Mongols. A leader with acute political instincts, Temujin launched a campaign to win over the tribes to his side. Those who still remained hostile were crushed in war. Within a period of five years, by 1189, Temujin subordinated all major tribes. In 1189 he was proclaimed Khan (King) of the Hamag Mongol *ulus*. In order to retain the loyalty of the feudal lords, Temujin instituted a system of privileges and titles. He knew that the old tribal rules were not good enough to cope with the administration of the enlarged state. So, he developed a sophisticated military structure of royal guards with unwavering loyalty and talent for intelligence gathering and alliances. The Tartars were the last tribe to be defeated, in 1205, paving the way for a unified state. The difficult process of unification and consolidation of the Mongol state has been described in great detail in the *Secret History of the Mongols*.

☞ FORMATION OF THE UNITED MONGOL STATE

In 1206, at the Great Hural (convention or gathering) of feudal princes and lords on the banks of Onon River, Temujin was proclaimed the supreme ruler of the unified Mongol state and conferred with the title of Chinggis Khan. The word 'Chinggis' comes from the Mongolian word *tengis*, or 'sea', while the word 'khan' means 'king'. Soon thereafter, Chinggis Khan introduced several new military-administrative reforms. The Mongolian state was divided into three principalities – the right, the left, and the central. Chinggis Khan retained the central unit under his direct rule, while the right and left units were governed by his prominent generals Mukhulai and Boorchu. The army was divided into units of *tumen*, or 10,000 horsemen. They were thereafter subdivided decimally right up to a count of ten. Each male member of the population was obliged to do military service.

Chinggis Khan introduced a code of laws called Ikh Zasag, written on white paper in a blue book. He mobilised 95,000 soldiers known as 95 *myangat*s, divided into 1,000 men each and headed by the *nohor* – always a close associate of the ruler. The army weaponry was primarily dominated by bows and arrows. Chinggis Khan also increased the number of his own bodyguards to 10,000.

The administration was based on the principles of 'military democracy'. Chinggis Khan constituted councils of leaders and intellectuals. Issues of national importance were decided by the Great Hural. Judges were appointed to administer the rule of law and decide on sentences. Theft and fraud were considered to be the gravest crimes. According to Persian historian Rashid-ad-Din, Chinggis Khan once said:

'Among the steppe people who are subject of my authority, theft, robbery and fornication were commonplace. Son did not obey father, young did not respect old, husband did not trust wife, wife ignored husband, rich did not help poor, junior did not respect senior, and, thus, the most unabashed disobedience and unlimited self-will dominated everywhere. I put an end to all this and established law and order among them.'

Thus, the unification of the Mongolian tribes and the establishment of a centralised state was an event of great significance in the history of the steppe people.

☙ THE LARGEST LAND EMPIRE

After reorganising his army and administration, Chinggis Khan decided to eliminate the threats from neighbouring rulers, who have always been at loggerheads with the Mongols. In 1209 he launched his first attack proper against the Tanguts, the traditional rivals of the Mongols, and turned them into a vassal state. In 1211 Chinggis Khan, accompanied by his four sons Zuchi, Tsagaadai, Ogodei and Tului, launched a military campaign against the powerful Chin dynasty in north-eastern China, and after a prolonged war in 1215 conquered its capital Beijing. This was a bloody war with thousands, perhaps millions, killed. With the fall of Beijing, Mongols gained control over the Silk Route linking China with other Central Asian states.

It is believed that at this stage Chinggis Khan had no ambition to expand his empire further, though he wanted access to trade routes with Khorezm, a prosperous Muslim state extending from Baghdad to present-day western China. He sent two separate missions to the Khorezm ruler Shah Muhammad for trade facilitation, but was rebuffed. Moreover, several of his emissaries were killed, and some were defaced and sent back. Following this diplomatic faux pas, Chinggis Khan invaded the state in 1221 and captured Turkestan, Bukhara, Samarkand, Urgench and parts of Persia. This was one of the bloodiest battles in history, leaving a trail of devastation. According to conservative estimates, over one million people were killed by the Mongol army during the war. Thereafter, continuing the military campaign against the fleeing Jalal-ad-Din, son of Shah Muhammad, Mongolian troops captured Afghanistan and reached the banks of Indus River in north-west India.

As the empire extended, Chinggis Khan needed an efficient communication system to maintain his command and control. He invented the 'Mongol Pony Post' with relay horses, with each horse covering about 30 kilometres at a time. The system enabled coverage of up to 600 kilometres in a day with 20 horses. What a remarkable achievement in those days!

The new frontiers created new threats — and those needed new wars. Interestingly, Chinggis Khan authorised new military campaigns in the bordering European states, but decided against invading India. Mongolian troops under the command of Zev and Subeedei invaded Azerbaijan and Georgia in 1221, and reached the Crimea, where the Mongol and Russian forces fought a fierce battle in May 1223 on the banks of the small Khalka River. In the aftermath of these wars, the Mongol Empire expanded as far west as the Black Sea.

GENGISKAN,

Grand Mogol.

Tiré en partie de la Voix Salomon.

A Paris chez Duflos rue St. Victor

A. P. D. R.

Having strayed too far from the nerve centre of the empire, Chinggis Khan asked his generals to turn back. He himself returned to Mongolia in 1225. The military expeditions to Central Asia, Persia, Afghanistan, north-western India and Russia left a horrible trail of death and devastation. For this reason many historians have described Chinggis Khan as 'the bloody invader'. In 1227, during yet another campaign against the resurfacing Tanguts, Chinggis Khan was wounded while hunting. The man who ruled the largest land empire died on 25 August 1227, at the age of 65. According to his instructions, his death and burial place were kept secret. Till date, his burial place remains a mystery.

⭗ OTHER KHANS

Subsequently, according to the departed ruler's wish, the empire was divided among his four sons. The divisions were not declared independent states, though, and were subject to the authority of the Great Hural. As decided by Chinggis Khan before his war against Khorezm, in 1229 the Great Hural elected his third son Ogodei as official successor and the second khan (1229–41). The other khans of the Mongol Empire were – Guyug Khan (1246–48), Munkh Khan (1251–59), and Kubilai Khan (1260–94).

Ogodei Khan reinforced the system of law and fair administration, and constructed Karakorum as the new capital. It was Ogodei who reportedly ordered the writing of the *Secret History of the Mongols*. He continued the policy of territorial expansion and sent troops to Persia (1230) and Caucasus (1231–39), while personally leading an expedition to crush the remnants of the Chin dynasty to complete the conquest of northern China. He also concluded a treaty with the Song dynasty in southern China and adopted the policy of religious freedom.

After Ogodei Khan's death in 1241, his widow Toregene took over as regent. Their son Guyug succeeded as the third khan in 1246. The accession ceremony was attended by Piano Carpini, a missionary of Pope Innocent IV, and several hundred representatives from Russia, China and Korea. Guyug's brief reign proved ineffective. Moreover, his election as khan was not approved by all the princes. Guyug died in 1248 in a military campaign against Batu Khan, another of the grandsons of Chinggis Khan.

Guyug was succeeded by Munkh Khan, son of Chinggis Khan's youngest son Tului. Munkh's election was not a smooth one either, with opposition from other descendants of Chinggis Khan including the Tsagaadai and Ogodei families. Soon after his election, Munkh used repressive tactics to consolidate his power. He and his brother Kubilai also launched a new military campaign to complete the conquest of China. Another brother Hulegu conquered Baghdad unseating the Abbasid caliph. Hulegu and his successors ruled large parts of the Middle East and Persia. After Munkh Khan's death in 1259, his brother Arigboh declared himself the next khan following a hurriedly convened Great Hural. Kubilai, in China at the time, challenged his brother's election and declared himself as khan, violating the well-established tradition of election.

Kubilai and Arigboh continued to wage several battles for supremacy, before Kubilai could emerge victorious. Kubilai did not stay in Karakorum, though. In 1267 he built his new capital called Khanbalig ('city of the Khan'), which forms part of present-day Beijing.

Facing page:
Chinggis Khan is recorded in history as the ruler of the largest-ever land empire.

32

Kubilai Khan moved the capital to Khanbalig to get access to major sea routes and Chinese resources – something that was not possible from Karakorum. Following Chinese tradition, he renamed his empire as Yuan dynasty in 1271. Although all religions were allowed to be practised, he declared Buddhism as state religion. Buddhist monks were granted special privileges. Mongolian was declared as state language.

Under Kubilai Khan, the Mongol Empire reached new heights with borders covering almost the whole of Asia and half of Europe. He also sent abortive military expeditions to Japan, Vietnam, Java and Burma. Inevitably, the administration became more and more difficult and complex. Although the overall control was in the hands of Mongols, Kubilai Khan made good use of Chinese administrative apparatus. Marco Polo in his memoirs provided a graphic account of the wealth and splendour of Kubilai Khan's court. During his rule, art and culture thrived and Buddhism became the religion of the masses. With the death of Kubilai Khan in 1294, once again the war of succession started. Between 1294 and 1330, there were nine emperors. In 1368 the last emperor Togoontumur Khan of Yuan dynasty was defeated by the Chinese (Ming dynasty) and driven back to Mongolia. Thus, Karakorum once again became the political centre of Mongolia.

Soldiers of the Chinese military forces.

Facing page:
Mongols besieging a citadel.

33

Erdene Zuu, a historic monastery, was set up on the ruins of the ancient Mongol city destroyed by the Chinese.

END OF MONGOL EMPIRE

The process of disintegration of the Mongol Empire started soon after the death of Kubilai Khan. The central authority weakened. Moreover, it was difficult to control the Mongolian tribes from the empire's nerve centre in Khanbalig. The peace achieved with China after the fall of Yuan dynasty did not last long. In 1380 the Chinese troops invaded Mongolia and burnt down large parts of Karakorum. Togstomor Khan, the then ruler of Mongolia, was himself killed leading to a war of succession. This led to complete chaos and feudal disintegration.

The anarchic conditions were fully exploited by the Ming rulers to take revenge against the Mongols for their subjugation of China. The Ming policy of that time is called 'Yi Yi Zhi Yi', or 'use some barbarians to govern others.' Consequently, several tribal lords of Mongolia became vassal states of Ming rulers. Around 1434, with the support of Ming China, the Oirad tribe – who in the past had fought against Chinggis Khan and his successors – rose to power and took control of most of Mongolian territory. Esen (1440–55) controlled almost all the land inhabited by Mongol tribes. However, his rule did not last long. He was killed during an uprising in 1455, once again plunging Mongolia into disintegration mode with several independent princedoms.

In 1470 Batmunkh, bestowed with the title Dayan Khan, acceded to the Mongolian throne. He attempted to unify the feudal lords, and also established peaceful relations with Ming China. However, after his death in 1543, the process of disintegration set in motion. Tumen Zasagt Khan, who ruled briefly after Dayan Khan, managed to hold the unity of the empire. He also accelerated the spread of Tibetan Buddhism throughout the country.

Dayan Khan's grandson Altan Khan was able to unite the feudal lords in Mongolia. He also concluded a peace treaty with Ming China in 1570, and opened border trade. Altan Khan promoted Lamaism. The historic monastery Erdene Zuu was set up in Karakorum on the ruins of the city destroyed by the Chinese. Eminent figures of that time were of the view that the spread of Buddhism in Mongolia would help in cessation of the feudal wars that had become almost regular. The last Mongol khan Ligden (1604–34), a descendant of Dayan Khan, tried his best to unify the feudal lords, but ultimately succumbed to Manchu rule.

ᏧᏲ MANCHU COLONISATION

The 275 years of Manchu rule are considered to constitute the darkest chapter in Mongolian history. At the time of Ligden Khan's defeat, Mongolia was divided into three major principalities – Inner Mongolia, Khalkh and Oirad. These were subdivided into many small, feudal possessions. Manchu rulers exploited this division by sharpening the wedge between them. Initially, the Manchu rulers acquired rights over the feudal lords to demote or punish them. A new code of conduct was prescribed. Manchu was declared the official language for correspondence.

Finally, after protracted wars and intermittent peace, in 1691 the princes of eastern and central Mongolia conferred in the city of Doloon Nuur and formally accepted Manchu rule in the presence of Manchu ruler Hangsi of Qing dynasty. Thus, central and eastern Mongolia was colonised, but it took several decades more to colonise western Mongolia, which continued to wage wars against Qing invaders under leaders such as Baatar Hontaij, Galdan Boshigt and Galdantseren. Mongolian historians have given graphic descriptions of Manchu atrocities. Most of them concur that the trail of devastation left behind by Chinggis Khan's military expeditions was not even a fraction of what the Manchus did. Manchu atrocities were characterised by torture, execution, forcible marriages of Mongolian women, corporal punishment, enslavement, and confiscation of livestock. Perhaps as a reaction to these atrocities, Mongolians turned towards God. New monasteries were constructed, and Lamaism became the religion of the masses. A large number of new literary works from India and Tibet were translated into Mongolian.

ᏧᏲ NATIONAL LIBERATION MOVEMENT

The oppressive policies pursued by the Manchu rulers led to widespread resentment and the eventual uprising against the Qing dynasty. The first such uprising was headed by the Oirad prince Amarsanaa in the mid-18th century. Another was led by the Hotgoid prince Chingunjav around the same time. However, the Manchu rulers were able to suppress these uprisings.

The largest popular uprising took place in Duguilan in Inner Mongolia, in the second half of the 19th century. Religious leaders led by Javzundamba Khutagt, Mongolia's eighth and last Bogd Khan (or Religious King), revolted against Manchu rule. These uprisings and protests in several parts of the country finally galvanised into the national liberation movement of 1911, leading to the overthrow of the Qing dynasty in Outer Mongolia.

The uprising against the Qing dynasty coincided with considerable warming of

Statue of Sukhbaatar, the hero of the revolution, in Ulaanbaatar. Engraved on the bottom of the statue are his words, 'If we, the whole people, unite in our common effort and common wealth, there will be nothing in the world that we cannot achieve, that we'll not have learnt or failed to do.'

relations between Mongolia and Russia. On 29 December 1911, Javzundamba VIII was crowned Head of Religion and State, and the state was named Mongolia. In 1912 there was an uprising in Inner Mongolia to join the newly constituted Mongolian state. This was, however, put down by the Chinese. Unfortunately, neither China nor tsarist Russia favoured complete independence to Mongolia. On 5 November 1913, a Russian-Chinese agreement was signed granting autonomy to Mongolia under Chinese suzerainty. Nevertheless, the Mongolian government under Prime Minister Sain Noyon Khan continued its efforts to secure Russian support for complete independence.

In 1915, a tripartite treaty was signed between Russia, China and Mongolia to restore statehood to Mongolia, though once again under Chinese suzerainty and Russian patronage. This aroused great indignation in Mongolia. Meanwhile, in October 1917 the people's revolution overthrew tsarist rule in Russia. The revolutionary government in Russia denounced all agreements signed with China and Japan concerning the status of Mongolia, and advocated full-fledged independence to Mongolia. In November 1919 the Chinese government, in violation of the treaty of 1915, sent armed forces to Mongolia. These developments naturally angered the Mongolians and the Russians, and led to another upsurge in the national liberation movement in Mongolia. The Mongolian masses no longer believed their feudal lords and they revolted both against feudalism and Chinese domination. In 1921 the Khalkha Mongols under the leadership of D. Sukhbaatar, D. Bodoo and S. Danzan, with the support of the Russian government, liberated Mongolian territory from Chinese occupation.

On 5 November 1921, an agreement for establishment of friendly relations between Mongolia and the Soviet Russia was signed in Moscow. All previous agreements signed with tsarist Russia were annulled. Between 1921 and 1924, various revolutionary changes were introduced, including abolition of feudalism and private ownership of land. In November 1924, the People's Great Hural approved the first Constitution of Mongolia. The country became a Soviet-style republic with a one-party system, which lasted until 1990. K. Choibalsan, Y. Tsedenbal and J. Batmunkh of the Mongolian People's Revolutionary Party dominated the Mongolian political scene during this period.

It was a period of considerable economic and social progress. Efforts were made towards industrial and agricultural development, eradication of illiteracy, and promotion of art and culture.

37

The Mongolian delegation secretary signs a treaty instituting diplomatic relations with Soviet Russia in November 1921.

Ulaanbaatar, Darkhan and Erdenet emerged as major cities, with more and more population converting from the nomadic to a settled life. However, the repressive regime of Soviet premier Stalin saw destruction of hundreds of monasteries, killing of thousands of Buddhist monks, as well as other brutalities that marked the darkest period of the Soviet era.

After a long period of the one-party system, the forces of democratic changes began to tug at the Mongolian heartland in the late 1980s. New political movements started under the leadership of the young and educated. Following the collapse of the Soviet Union, Mongolians shifted to democracy in July 1990. A new constitution was adopted in January 1992. Parliamentary and presidential elections have each been held four times since then. Today, Mongolia stands as an emerging multiparty democracy overseen by peaceful change of governments. People enjoy all fundamental freedoms including those of speech and faith. Since 1990, Mongolia has also taken steps to make the transition to a free market economy.

Left: Horsemen in traditional dress on Mongolian National Day.

Below: A plaza in front of a department store in Ulaanbaatar.

GEOGRAPHY AND NATURE

Mongolia is a landlocked country, located between the Russian Federation in the north and China in the south. The country shares 3,485 kilometres of border with Russia and 4,677 kilometres with China. Mongolia is the nineteenth largest country in the world – nearly three times the size of France and almost five times that of the United Kingdom. With an average altitude of 1,580 metres above sea level, Mongolia is one of the highest countries in the world. The highest point is Huiten Orgil in Altai Range in Bayan-Ulgii aimag, at 4,374 metres; the lowest point is the Khar Nuur depression in Dornod aimag, at 532 metres. For administrative purposes the country is divided into 21 aimags. Mongolia is one of the few countries almost untouched by human development (or destruction). By and large, the landscape is virgin and flaunts spectacular beauty. The country is endowed with high mountain ranges with glaciers, vast steppe grasslands, semi-arid and super-arid deserts, and beautiful lakes and rivers.

Left: The Ahgii Mountains form a natural barrier marking the border between Mongolia and Tuva.

Below: Over the ages, the Tsaatan people have bred strong and docile reindeer.

Mongolia is characterised by a harsh continental climate with very low precipitation, long winters, and short summers. The average temperature in winter months is -20°C and in summers it is +20°C. The January temperature ranges between -32°C and -53°C, while the July temperature lies between +28°C and +43°C. The annual average precipitation is around 220 millimetres. Of the four seasons, spring (March-May) is the most unpredictable. The weather conditions could vary considerably within a day – from snowfall to strong winds, or to high temperatures. Marked by very low humidity, the air is fairly dry all over the country.

✎ MOUNTAINOUS REGION

The country is divided into three distinct geographical regions. The mountainous region in the northern and western parts has several high peaks that are perpetually snow-covered. The central and eastern parts are steppe grasslands, while the vast Gobi Desert forms most of southern Mongolia. The Altai, the Khangai, the Huvsgul and the Khentii mountain ranges constitute the mountainous region of the north and the west.

The Altai Mountains in the western part of the country stretch up to 650 kilometres, and are comparatively thin hills with high peaks. There are 190 glaciers in the highest parts of these mountains, with a total size of about 540 square kilometres including the 19-kilometre-long Potanin Glacier. In the centre of the country the Khangai Range divides Asia's continental watershed. East of Ulaanbaatar lies the rugged Khentii Mountains – where Chinggis Khan was born. Huvsgul Mountains are located to the west of Huvsgul Lake.

Lake near Hovd, Bayan-Ulgii, western Mongolia.

Preceding pages 42-43:
Road to Hustai Nuruu Steppe Reserve.

45

While the Altai and Huvsgul ranges are steep, the Khangai and Khentii are wide and defined by high plateaus. Most of the high peaks are located in the Altai and Khangai ranges. There are 29 mountain peaks with an altitude of over 3,000 metres. Mountain peaks over 4,000 metres are: Huiten in Bayan-Ulgii (4,374 metres), Munkh Khairhan in Hovd (4,204 metres), Tsambagarav in Bayan-Ulgii (4,195 metres), Tast in Bayan-Ulgii (4,193 metres), Sutai in Gobi Altai (4,090 metres), Kharkhiraa in Uvs (4,037 metres), Otgon Tenger in Zavkhan (4,021 metres), and Takhiltyn in Bayan-Ulgii (4,019 metres). The climate in the mountainous region is characterised by extreme cold and strong winds. This zone is characterised by tundra and alpine-sedge meadows, highland swamps and boulder fields. Contiguous to the mountainous region runs Mongolia's taiga zone with dense forests. The coniferous forests constitute about six per cent of Mongolian territory, and provide much-needed timber as well as help sustain the country's ecosystem. This region also receives comparatively higher precipitation at nearly 400 millimetres per annum.

✇ STEPPE ZONE

Steppe grassland makes up the central and far eastern parts of the country. Varying from gently rolling terrain to areas quite as flat as a table, the steppe grassland and mountain steppes cover more than 40 per cent of Mongolian territory. The second largest steppe in the world, the Menen Steppe with a length of over 200 kilometres, is located in Dornod in the far-eastern part of Mongolia. The mountain steppe zone – occurring where the taiga meets the steppes – is characterised by maximum biodiversity and a large number of rivers and lakes.

The Mongolian steppe region is the most populated part of the country. The grasslands support millions of domestic animals.

Facing page: *Rivers and lakes recur through the mountain steppe zone.*

This region in the lower elevation of the Altai, Khangai and Khentii mountains is habitat to a large number of wild animals and rare species of birds.

The steppe region is the most populated part of the country. The grasslands provide pasture to millions of domestic animals and, thus, have a major role in sustaining the nomadic way of life. The steppes in the south-east, though, are primarily uninhabited due to extremely arid conditions. Nevertheless, they do provide an undisturbed home to hundreds of thousands of Mongolian gazelles and migratory birds.

THE GOBI

Ancient fossils clearly indicate that the vast Gobi Desert was once a part of a vast inland sea. Though starkly beautiful, the fabled Gobi is rugged and inhospitable. It occupies most of the southern part of Mongolia, bordering China. Precipitation is very low and vegetation, sparse. The Gobi is characterised by rocky mountains, vast flatland, super-arid desert, oases, and sand dunes. Since the region is hostile to human existence, population remains very sparse. There are areas for hundreds of kilometres without trace of human habitat. With vast areas of the Gobi devoid of trees, mountains, or human habitat, one gets an infinite view until horizons – as on the high seas.

The dunes of the Gobi loom over herders' gers.

Right: *Camels tamed in the desert are of the two-hump (Bactrian) variety.*

The climate in the Gobi is extreme. Temperatures vary from -40°C to +40°C, with precipitation less than 100 millimetres per annum. During spring, desert storms with a velocity of 140 kilometres per hour are quite common. Despite such hostile conditions, Mongolian Gobi provides habitat to several threatened animal species such as wild camel, Gobi bear, wild sheep, wild ass and black-tailed antelopes. South Gobi, or Umn Govi, with its vast sand dunes and infinite horizons is certainly the most beautiful province in Gobi Desert. The Hongor sand dunes in South Gobi are 185 kilometres long and 20 kilometres wide. With mountains in the backdrop and a stream in front, they provide a magnificent sight. The whistling sound of those sand dunes creates amazing musical effects.

Given its unique landscape, the Gobi has also been a subject of several ancient legends. According to one such legend, once upon a time a Mongolian tribal chief was forced to leave his town by the Chinese army. The chief, being skilled in the art of black magic – a Shamanist tradition, uttered some black word that made the land shrivel and die behind him, leaving nothing for the Chinese but a vast arid land with hardly any trace of vegetation. This became the great Gobi Desert!

❧ LAKES

Several beautiful lakes adorn the vast landscape of Mongolia. They constitute one of the most important elements of the country's geography. The Huvsgul Lake in Huvsgul aimag bordering

Lake Huvsgul, the second largest freshwater lake in Asia.

Russia is the second largest freshwater lake in Asia, with low mineralisation. It is 136 kilometres long and covers a total area of 2,760 square kilometres. It has an average width of 36.5 kilometres and a maximum depth of 262 metres. Huvsgul Lake is the 14th largest source of fresh water in the world, with storage of two per cent of the world's fresh water. More than 90 rivers flow into the lake, but only one – the Eg – flows out.

Uvs Lake covering a total area of 3,350 square kilometres is the largest lake in Mongolia. The lake is 84 kilometres long with a total shoreline of 425 kilometres. The average width is 40 kilometres and the average depth, 12 metres. This is a saltwater lake with very high mineral contents – five times as high as seawater. This is also the country's coldest region with a recorded temperature of -58°C. Uvs Lake is on the World Heritage List of UNESCO.

Khar-Us Lake in the Hovd aimag is the country's third largest lake, with a total area of 1,852 square kilometres. It has a length of 72 kilometres, an average width of 27 kilometres, and an average depth of only 4 metres. It is a freshwater lake with low mineral contents. Other important lakes of Mongolia include Khyargas Lake in Hovd aimag (1,407 square kilometres), Buir Lake in Dornod aimag (615 square kilometres), and Terkhiin Tsagaan Lake in Arhangai aimag (61 square kilometres).

❧ RIVERS AND SPRINGS

Mongolia has over 3,800 rivers and streams, with a total length of 67,000 kilometres. The country is also endowed with about 6,900 springs including many sulphur springs and spa resorts. Several of them are known for their curative properties.

The rivers belong to three different basins – the Arctic Basin, the Pacific Ocean Basin, and the Central Asian Inland Basin. The three big rivers Selenge, Orkhon and Tuul belong to the Arctic Basin. The Selenge is the principal river of the country – it is about 1,024 kilometres long and has a drainage area of approximately 282,050 square kilometres in Mongolian territory. It

Tsagaan Nuur depression, northern Mongolia.

drains into Lake Baikal in Russia. The Orkhon, with a length of about 1,124 kilometres and a drainage area of some 132,855 square kilometres, is the most important tributary of the Selenge. The rivers Tuul and Kharaa drain into Orkhon.

The Onon, Kherlen and Khalkh are the major rivers in eastern Mongolia and form part of the Pacific Ocean Basin. These rivers, with a length of about 2,000 kilometres in Mongolian territory, are the only source of water in the Khentii and Dornod provinces. Onon river, which drains into the mighty Amur, has a total length of 298 kilometres in Mongolian territory. The Kherlen, running about 1,090 kilometres in Mongolian territory, originates in Khentii Mountains and drains into Lake Dalai in China. The Khalkh, with a total length of 233 kilometres, drains into Lake Buir.

The Bulgan, Hovd and Zarkhan are the major rivers in the Central Asian Inland Basin. The Bulgan and the Hovd originate in Altai Mountains, while the Zavkhan springs from the Khangai range.

ᨶ FLORA AND FAUNA

Once upon a time, thousands of dinosaurs roamed on Mongolian territory. Many fossils, skeletons and eggs of those dinosaurs have been found in the South Gobi area. Some of these can be seen in the Natural History Museum in Ulaanbaatar.

Since the Mongolian environment is, on the whole, still unspoilt – mainly due to the nomadic culture of preservation of nature, the very low density of population, and the relatively late onset of mining and industrialisation – the flora and fauna remain robust. The country is habitat to about 140 mammal species, of which 45 are listed as very rare and prohibited for hunting. These include Gobi bear (Ursus pruinosis), wild ass, wild camel (Camalus bactrianus), Takhi horse (Equus przewalski), elk, sable, small deer (khuder) and Asian beaver. Among other important mammal species found in Mongolia are – wild boar, wild

Przewalski's horse mare and foal.

sheep, wild goat, northern deer, musk deer, maral stag, roe, fox, corsac, lynx, ermine, Siberian weasel, snow leopard, wolf, gazelle, antelope, marmot or tarbaga, mazaalai bear, racoon dog, stoat and muskrat.

Taki Horse

The Takhi, or Przewalski's, horses are the last remaining wild horses in the world. These horses have 66 chromosomes compared to 64 in normal breed of horses. It is believed that in the 18th and 19th centuries, there were thousands of Takhi horses in Mongolia. This number declined considerably due to increasing pressure on pastures. The last wild Mongolian Takhis were found in the western Gobi in 1966.

Subsequently, due to the collaborative efforts of Mongolian Association for Conservation of Nature and Environment and the Dutch Foundation Reserves of Przewalski Horses, these horses were reintroduced in Mongolia in 1992. Presently, the population of Takhi horses is estimated around 200. Most of them are in the protected areas of Hustai Nuruu (100 kilometres from Ulaanbaatar), Bugat soum of Govi-Altai, and the Khamin Tal buffer zone of Khar-Us Nuur National Park.

For the nomads, animals are a source of food (meat, milk), clothing (wool, cashmere, hide), housing (felt, rope, carpet), transportation, and even sport (horse race, camel race, polo).

Wild Ass, or Khulan

The wild ancestors of the present-day ass are common in the desert and desert steppes in Mongolia. The khulans live in herds of as many as 500 and they can run up to 65 kilometres per hour. The Gobi's wild ass population is the largest among the four sub-population groups of the Asiatic wild ass. Dzungarian Gobi, close to the border of China, is the principal habitat for most of the wild asses of Mongolia.

Wild Sheep and Goat

The largest living wild sheep, the argali, is found in the Altai, Khangai, Khuvsgul and Khentii mountains. It has unusually long and big horns, with the length of a fully grown argali anywhere between 160 and 180 centimetres. The argali is around 122 centimetres high and weighs up to 200 kilograms.

One species of wild goat, the yangir (Capra sibirica), is found in large numbers in the Mongolian mountains. The yangir is about 100 centimetres high, 75 centimetres long, and up to 130 kilograms heavy. Both the argali and the yangir are extremely good climbers.

Snow Leopard

The snow leopard is the only species among the big cats adapted to cold zones. It lives with wild sheep and wild goats in the high and rocky mountains. It feeds on small mammals, particularly marmot, roe deer and red deer. The fur coat of the snow leopard is highly prized by hunters for its value in the market. The population of the animal – listed in the IUCN Red Data Book as endangered – in Mongolia is estimated to be about 1,200.

Birds

According to the latest statistics, 434 species of birds belonging to 193 genres, 56 families and 17 orders have been registered in Mongolia. While 330 of these are migratory birds, the rest 104 inhabit Mongolia throughout the year. The principal habitat for these birds are the large Mongolian lakes such as Uvs, Khuvsgul, Khar-Us, Terkhin Tsagaan, Buir and Khargo. The rare bird species found in Mongolia include Siberian crane, white-napped crane, houbara bustard, black stork, Dalmatian pelican, white spoonbill, Baikal teal, Asiatic dowitcher, mountain ouzel, wood grouse, water fowl, white-tailed sea eagle, hawk, falcon, harrier, black griffon and snow cock.

Gobi Bear

The Gobi bear, or the mazaalai, is an endangered species found only in the Altai Gobi region. It is estimated that only around 20 of these bears are left. The bear is comparatively small, with body length of 155-167 centimetres and height of 92-110 centimetres. Some scholars are of the view that it is a sub-species of the greasy bear found in Canada and Mexico.

Fish

Since there is no commercial fishing in Mongolia, the rivers and lakes are a paradise for anglers. It is believed that up to 750 tonnes of fish can be caught annually from the lakes and rivers. The main fish varieties are salmon, trout, sturgeon, green fish, grayling and white fish. The Amur sturgeon, the Siberian sturgeon, the glass carp and the silver carp are listed as endangered. Large numbers of western tourists visit Mongolia mainly on fishing expeditions.

Flora

Given the vast size of the country, the varied nature of its geography, and the different levels of precipitation, Mongolia has diverse and distinctive vegetation. Plant species of Siberian Taiga, the Central Asian steppes, the fertile river valleys, and the semi-arid and super-arid deserts are all found in Mongolia. According to available statistics, there are 845 species of medicinal plants, over 1,000 species of fodder plants, 173 species of food plants, and 490 species of ornamental plants. Classified by the seeding varieties of plants, 2,095 species are herbaceous and 348 species are woody and shrubby. Of these, 128 plant species are registered as endangered.

Forests cover over 8 per cent of Mongolian territory. The lower parts of the northern and western mountainous region have dense forests. Coniferous and broad-leaf forests occupy about 84 per cent of forest reserves in the country.

Strictly Protected

The country has 12 strictly protected areas covering 40,000 square kilometres of area, in addition to seven national parks and 13 national reserves. These are places that may be of historic importance, or that contain unique natural formations of spectacular beauty, or that provide habitat to rare animal and bird species. Strictly protected areas include Bogd Mountain, Great Gobi Strictly Protected Area, Eastern Steppes, Uvs Lake Basin, Mongol Daguur and Khokh Serkh. Important national parks include Huvsgul Lake, Khargo White Lake, Gobi Gurvansaikhan, Terelj National Park and Khangai Nuruu. Some of the prominent national reserves are Batkhaan Uul, Bulgan River Area, Hustai Nuruu, Nagalkhaan Uul, Ugtam Mountain and Yol Valley.

The land has an abundance of flower varieties including anemone crinita, delphinium, iris and milk thissle.

Facing page: Reindeer crossing a stream.

Following pages 60-61: Mongolia's flora includes nearly 150 endemic plants and about 100 relic species. More than 100 plant species are officially categorised as rare or endangered.

Ρ EOPLE

At the end of 2005, Mongolian population was estimated at 2.6 million – approximately four times that of 1918. The population density of Mongolia is 1.5 people per square kilometre, making it the most sparsely populated country in the world. There are more than 20 ethnic groups in Mongolia, with the Khalkha constituting over 80 per cent of the total population. The Kazakh, who primarily live in the western aimag (state) of Bayan-Ulgii, make up about six per cent of the population. Other ethnic groups include Barga, Bayat, Buriyat, Dharkhad, Dorvod, Myagnad, Tsaatan, Uuld, Torguud, Uriankhai and Zakhchin. About 45 per cent of Mongolians presently live in the three major cities – Ulaanbaatar, Darkhan and Erdenet. Nonetheless, nomadism continues to remain a predominant way of life in the vast territory of Mongolia. Harsh climatic conditions, very low precipitation, and poor fertility of soil play an important role in dictating the nomadic way of life.

The Mongolian language belongs to the Altai group of languages – as do Turkish, Kazakh and Uzbek. Mongolian writing system does not correspond to the pronunciation. Moreover, the script has changed several times – Pags-pa in 1269, Todu in 1648, Soyombo in 1686, and Cyrillic in 1941.

Young Mongolian women in their traditional dress.

Below: *Double wood or dung burning stove is used for cooking and occupies the central position in a ger.*

❧ HERDING

Herding and hunting are a traditional way of life among the nomads. Horse, cattle, yak, camel, sheep and goat are the six most important animals, in that order. This is also called the hierarchy or aristocracy of animals. The horse is considered to be the most important as it provides mobility, speed and power. Among horses, the white horse is regarded as the best. The yak is found in high-altitude, hilly areas, while the camel inhabits the Gobi Desert. Mongolian camels are of the two-hump (Bactrian) variety.

The total animal population in Mongolia is approximately 32 million. The wealth of a nomad is calculated on the basis of the number of animals he owns. Although pastures are common property, and remain non-demarcated, these are traditionally associated with nomadic families and tribes with grazing rights. Other tribes or families are not allowed to use them. Even while the nomads move from one place to another

The horse is considered to be the most important animal as it provides mobility and speed.

Left: *A Mongolian family with their camels. They live in the very sparsely populated aimag of South Gobi.*

A Kazakh eagle hunter in
western Mongolia. The
Kazakhs have mastered
the art of hunting with
eagles, the skill inherited
from their Turkic ancestors
and passed on through
generations.

in the summer and winter months, they retain their traditional rights over these pastures. For identification of their animals, people have evolved an elaborate system of stamping them.

The life of a nomad primarily revolves around his animals. They are a source of food (meat and milk), clothing (wool, cashmere and hide), housing (felt, ropes and carpets), transportation and even sport (horse race, camel race and polo). Along with herding, hunting is considered to be an essential part of nomadic lifestyle. Hunting is not only a sport, but also a source of food as well as goods that can be traded (fur and skin). Most important, it is also a training in the art of fighting the enemy. Besides, hunting of wolf is considered essential to protect herds.

Since nature plays an extremely important role in the life of the nomads, Mongolians are very conscious of their environment and, hence, do not hunt indiscriminately. Moreover, a large number of animals and birds are considered sacred and forbidden for hunting.

Mongolian woman tending to her cattle.

Right: *Meat and milk remain the most important sources of diet. Fish from the rivers are yet another source of food.*

POLO IN THE STEPPES

Passion for horses is as ancient as the origin of humanity itself. The power and speed of horses have always fascinated human beings. The number and breed of horses have been a symbol of power for kings and feudal lords both in Europe and Asia. Nobody knows the precise origin of polo, but the game obviously came as an offshoot of horse race and other horse sports. Arabs, Persians, Indians and Europeans share a long history of horse races. Central Asia is considered to be the birthplace of polo or a variant of it, though there has been no conclusive proof of it.

According to historical records, a variant of present-day polo did exist in Mongolia in the 12th and 13th centuries. Chinggis Khan, who organised a large-scale professional cavalry, used polo as a training sport. The horsemen were trained to bend their bodies like an acrobat and shoot arrows while riding at high speed. They were also taught body manoeuvres to protect themselves against enemy arrows, to attack the fallen enemies, and to take away their weapons and other possessions while still riding at high speed. During the course of extended wars, the army also used to hit the fallen enemy heads like a ball as recreation. Moreover, when the Chinggis empire expanded from the Pacific Ocean in the east to the Black Sea in the west, the king needed an effective communication system to receive reports and intelligence, and to issue instructions and commands. For this, he established a relay postal system on horseback throughout his empire, with one horseman covering a distance of 30 kilometres in an hour. Efficient functioning of this system needed proper training of horses and horsemen. So, the emperor introduced a system of training on horseback at a young age. Children above six years of age were taught acrobatic manoeuvres on horseback, done in the form of a sport similar to present-day polo.

Although horse race continued to remain an essential feature of life in the steppes, the game of polo or its variant was largely forgotten after the fall of the Mongol Empire in the 14th century. As a result, today polo is not a popular sport in Mongolia, though efforts are underway to revive it. These efforts have been reinforced as Mongolia celebrates the 800th anniversary of the Mongol Empire this year. Mongolian Polo Federation and Chinggis Khan Polo Club are making all-out efforts to rejuvenate the sport in Mongolia.

Apart from horse polo, camel polo is also emerging in Mongolia in recent times. The country is habitat to over 250,000 Bactrian camels. Camel polo festival is held every year in February/March in the Gobi region. The camel polo festival for 2006 was held in Dundgobi aimag with participation of 31 Mongolian teams and one Chinese team as well. The Mongolian Association of Camel Polo is promoting the sport in Mongolia. Also, in 2006 yak polo was launched for the first time. The first game was held on 20 June 2006, in Ulaanbaatar. Since yak population in Mongolia is decreasing at an alarming pace, the sport was launched to create awareness about the need to preserve the habitat of this animal.

Polo was a favoured sport in medieval Asia. Princes from China to Persia indulged in it, while Chinggis Khan used polo to train his cavalry.

❧ FOOD

The food habits of the nomads are primarily guided by herding and hunting, as also by the harsh climatic conditions they live in. Meat and milk remain the most important sources of diet. The domesticated animals that the nomads slaughter for cooking are the sheep and the cow. Horses are killed only for very special occasions. Among the foods obtained from hunting are rabbit, deer, wild pig and marmot. Fish from the rivers, as well as the milk of mare, cow and sheep are other important sources of food. Fermented mare's milk – *airag*, fermented cow's milk – *esug*, homemade yogurt – *tarag*, Mongolian hot, salty tea – *suutai chai*, dried cheese made of curdled milk – *aaruul*, thick layer of white butter – *urum*, and alcohol made of mare's milk – *kumis*, are important milk products. They are also called white products as all of them are derived from milk. Some of the traditional and most popular food items among the nomads are fried meat patties – *huushuur*, lamb meat wrapped in flattened dough and steamed – *buuz*, lamb pieces cooked with hot stones – *khorkhog*, skinned carcass of goat filled with hot stones and barbecued – *boodog*, and flour cookies fried in oil – *boortsog*.

In ancient times, alcoholic beverages of the Mongols were restricted to *airag* and *kumis*. According to historical records, Chinggis Khan was opposed to habitual and excessive drinking. He is reported to have said:

'A drunkard is like one who is blind, deaf and insane; he cannot even stand erect, but is like a man that is struck upon the head. Regardless of what talent or training a person may have, to the drunkard these things are useless; all he will receive from others is insults. The ruler who becomes addicted to wine can never undertake a great enterprise. A general who likes wine can never control his troops. Whoever it may be who has this evil habit, it will certainly lead to disaster.'

A Mongolian woman lays cheese on the roof of her yurt.

Facing page:
Top: *Tsaatan children eating reindeer meat and bone.*
Below: *Woman drying reindeer meat.*

Since the development of close ties between Mongolia and the Soviet Union in the early 20th century, vodka has become the most popular drink. It is nearly like a national drink and is used on all festive and ceremonial occasions. Of late, beer and wine are also becoming popular among the younger generation in cities.

Food habits in the cities – in Ulaanbaatar prominently – are changing as well, with more use of vegetables, rice and fruits. With the opening of numerous pubs, bars and restaurants – particularly since the mid-1990s – and the growing prosperity of the people, they tend to eat out more often than before.

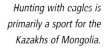
CLOTHING

For Mongols, protection from the extreme cold and the strong winds, freedom when riding horses, and suitable coverings when camping out in the wilderness, are essential elements of clothing. Mongolians like to wear richly decorated clothes with considerable attention to details. Traditionally, Chinese silk and cotton cloth are used for making dresses. *Del*, *terleg*, *khurem*, *gutal*, and a colourful variety of headgears are important traditional items of clothing.

The *del* is the conventional garment of the Mongols. It is a long, loose gown cut in one piece. It has a high collar and a wide overlap at the front. The *del* is girdled with a sash. Each ethnic group in Mongolia has its own style of *del* distinguished by cut, colour and trimming. *Del*s for men and women are of the same cut, except that male *del*s are wider and of more demure colours. The *del* for everyday wear is grey or brown, and made in less expensive silk or cotton; the one for festive occasions is made in expensive, rich and decorated silk, with a silk sash of contrasting colours. Festive *del*s are in bright colours like blue, purple and red. The *terleg* is a slightly padded *del*. For the winter, the *del* is padded with sheepskin or wool. In cold weather a jacket known as *khurem* is worn over the *del* for protection. The *gutal* is a high

Hunting with eagles is primarily a sport for the Kazakhs of Mongolia.

Facing page:
The del *is the traditional garment of the Mongols. It is a long, loose gown with a high collar and wide overlap at the front.*

Portrait of three Mongolian women in traditional clothes. The two on the right are wives of district petty officials. The one on the left is unmarried.

boot made from leather and lined with fine, thin felt. They are also decorated with different motifs and designs.

One of the most colourful items of Mongolian dress is the traditional headgear. The most fashionable brands in headwear would be dazzled by the sheer variety of headgears in Mongolia. There are hats for the young and the old, for men and women, for summers and winters, and for daily wear and special occasions. Moreover, each ethnic group has its distinctive features on headgears. They are made in fur, leather, silk, or velvet – or even in a mix of all these. The shapes could be conical, cubical, cylindrical, spherical, or a combination of all these. Most of the headgears are decorated with corals, pearls, or other adornments. There are over 100 varieties of headgears in Mongolia. The Ku-Ku, Shibulger and Mount Sumber are some of the most popular varieties.

Mongolians are fond of jewellery and are well-known for their artwork in creating beautiful pieces of jewellery in gold, silver and semi-precious stones. The women wear beautiful items of jewellery, while the men pride in wearing the *khet khutga* – a set of finger pouch and knife. A richly decorated knife with handle and sheath made of silver, leather, or wood, is the prized possession of a man.

Above: Men hammering designs into silver bowls.
Below: Silverwork boots with gold pattern.

Facing page:
Top: Silver platter.
Below: Bronze plaque.

With time, the traditional way of clothing is becoming an extinct commodity in the big cities in Mongolia. Most men and women in the cities prefer western-style clothing. Even marriage ceremonies are held in the western-style long, white gowns. It is mainly on festive or ceremonial occasions that city dwellers apparently prefer traditional costumes. Traditional clothing, of course, remains the norm for nomadic families even today.

ᴥ MONGOLIAN DWELLING

The Mongolian word *ger* for their ancient dwelling seems to have its origin in the Sanskrit word *grih*, or *ghar*, meaning 'house'. The Mongolian *ger* is a scientifically developed dwelling to suit the nomadic way of life and the harsh climatic conditions, and has, therefore, survived thousands of years of scientific innovations. Even with the development of cities, the *ger* continues to remain the principal mode of dwelling in Mongolia. This is light and collapsible, and can withstand temperatures from -50°C to +50°C, heavy snow and strong winds. The walls are made from thin birch willows formed into a lattice (*khana*) and held together by leather strips. Several sections of the lattice are put together into a large circular wall. The size of the *ger* depends on the number of *khana*s used. Six to eight *khana*s make for an average

Mongols building the traditional ger. *Roof stringers are tied to the expandable lattice side walls. The canvas and the felt covering are attached next. An ordinary-size* ger *can be erected within 45 minutes, and dismantled even quicker.*

Previous pages 82-83: *One of the most colourful items of the traditional Mongolian costume is the headgear. There is an amazing array of headgears that Mongolians sport.*

Transporting a ger *on a cart. Mongolians transport their* ger *every time they move!*

size. For ceremonial purposes and for feudal lords, giant *ger*s are prepared from 12 to 24 *khana*s. An ordinary-size *ger* can be erected within 45 minutes, and this can be dismantled even quicker! The *ger* can also be erected on a moving platform – as was done by the soldiers of Chinggis Khan. Nomads transport their *ger*s every time they move. This was earlier done on camels and horses, but these days trucks are routinely used.

The ceiling of the *ger* is formed from an umbrella-like frame of poles called *uni*. There is an opening in the centre of the ceiling called *toono*. This allows smoke to escape and fresh air and sunlight to come in. The *uni* and the *toono* hold the *ger* together. In the centre of the *ger* is the hearth, or *golomt*, symbolising ties with ancestors. In winter the hearth heats the *ger* and also serves as cooking stove. This is regarded as the most sacred area since fire is sacred to Mongols. The entire outside surface of the *ger* is covered with felt and is tied with woollen ropes. The layers of felt can be increased or reduced depending upon the outside temperature. The Mongolian *ger* always faces south, mainly because the cold winds come from the north. Thus, the door also serves as compass in this land of vast expanse, infinite horizons and few people. The furnishings of *ger*s are quite simple with a standard variety of chests, centre table, stools and beds. Felt, rugs and carpets are used on the floor.

Mongolians are very particular about *ger* etiquettes as these are associated with traditions, superstitions and taboos. For instance, it is considered bad manners to knock on the door. Instead, one should call *Nokhoi hori*, or 'May I come in'. After crossing the threshold, the man should move to the left and the woman to the right. One should never step on the threshold as it is considered tantamount to stepping on the neck of the owner. Towards the back and a little to the west is the place of honour set aside for guests. The back of the *ger*, directly opposite the entrance, is the *khoimor* – the place set aside for elders and the most honoured. On the back wall is the family altar with Buddhist images. On the male side are saddles and big leather bags for milk and *airag*, and on the female side are the cooking implements. Some of these arrangements may vary slightly, depending upon the tribal traditions. Thus, the chimney of Kazakh *ger*s is to the right side of the *toono*, while in the Mongol *ger*s it is to the left. Mongolians are good hosts and known for their hospitality. As soon as you enter you will be offered *suutai chai*, *aaruul*, *urum* and *boortsog*. In summer you will be offered *airag*, *tarag* and other milk products. Thereafter, vodka and freshly cooked *buuz* are offered. When you leave, you should walk out the way you entered.

With growing prosperity and modernisation, there have been some new additions. These days the *ger*s of rich nomads are equipped with television, dish antenna, cooking range, microwave oven, refrigerator and solar panels for electricity. Quite a few of them also have motorbikes and cars. In *soum* (administrative unit, like a district) centres where cell signals are available, cellphones are common. There are interesting scenes that make for a fascinating melange of the traditional and the modern – for instance, scenes of people riding their horses to reach right up to the entrance of an aircraft to board the flight!

The gers *of rich nomads come equipped with television and dish antenna these days.*

Following pages 88-89 :
Ethnic Mongols account for about 85 per cent of the total population. The Khalkha make up more than 80 per cent of the total ethnic population.

SOCIAL MORES

Through the centuries, Mongolians have considered the education of their children an essential part of upbringing. In the olden times, knowledge and values were imparted by members of the family through oral transmission. Proverbs and stories were widely used for transmission of wisdom. Puzzles and toys were used for sharpening the child's intellect. The Intellectual Museum in Ulaanbaatar, with its wide-ranging collection of puzzles and games, is a testimony to this strong tradition.

From the beginning of the 20th century, a large number of kindergartens and schools have been opened all over the country. Although the population is widely dispersed, about 96 per cent of Mongolians are literate and over 65 per cent possess university degrees. Children from remote areas are usually sent to Ulaanbaatar for higher education. Equality of the male child and the female child is an important element of Mongolian traditions. In recent years Mongolian women have been excelling in all walks of life. Nearly 70 per cent of university students are female. Most offices have more female than male

Equality of the male and the female child is an important aspect of Mongolian traditions. The education of their children is accorded due priority by the Mongolians.

Following pages 92-93 :
Mongolian children jumping into the water.

In recent years, Mongolian women have been excelling in several disciplines. Nearly 70 per cent of university students are estimated to be female.

workers. Mongolians also share considerable interest in music, dance, singing, painting, poetry and sports, and are reputed as extremely talented in mathematics and logic. Chess is one of the most popular sports in Mongolia.

The *khadag*, a blue or white silk scarf, is extensively used as a sign of respect for elders. Ayush *khadag*s with figures of the Buddha are given to elders, parents and highly regarded guests, while nanjvandan *khadag*s with symbols of the sun and the moon are offered for burial ceremonies. The *khadag* must always be triple-folded and its open side directed towards the receiver. *Khadag*s are also offered to deities at monasteries, or placed at *ovoo*s (Shamanic shrines) and other holy places. Some trees regarded as holy are also offered the *khadag*.

The snuffbox has an important place in Mongolian society. After the guests take their seats, they are offered the snuffboxes. Snuffboxes are passed with the lids slightly open, on the upturned palm of the right hand. One can open it or just sniff at the half-open lid, and pass it further. Snuffboxes are considered a family treasure in Mongolia and they are passed on from generation to generation. Rich people even try to outdo each other in the style, design and size of their snuffboxes. Snuffboxes are generally made of chalcedony, jade, jasper, agate, or turquoise, and are decorated with carved figures like those of Garuda, the lion, the dragon, and the tiger.

☞ TSAGAAN SAR – LUNAR NEW YEAR

Tsagaan Sar, the White Month or the Lunar New Year, is one of the two most important festivals in Mongolia; the other one is Naadam. According to the Central Asian lunar calendar, Tsagaan Sar falls sometime between the end of January and early March. There are several explanations for the celebration. Some say it symbolises the end of winter and the beginning of spring, thereby implying a time of happiness and prosperity. Some believe it marks the beginning of the lactating and breeding period, which is very important in the life of a nomad. According to another viewpoint, the word has been derived from *tsagaa* (milk product) as it was customary to eat only milk products during the festival month. This view also holds that in ancient times Tsagaan Sar used to be celebrated in August/September. There is another explanation still – in 1206, to celebrate his new title of the Great Khan, Temujin organised a massive feast in the beginning of spring, and since then it became customary to celebrate the New Year in the beginning of spring.

Preparations for Tsagaan Sar start at least a month in advance. *Gers*, apartments and houses are cleaned. New clothes and gifts are bought. Hundreds of *buuz* are prepared. Some families prepare over 2,000 *buuz*! A circular arrangement of special bread, *ul boov*, is prepared on a table or a big plate in layers of three, five, or nine. Nine layers are prepared for state ceremonies and by very important people, and three by young couples. Most others prepare five layers. The top of *ul boov* is decorated with sweets, sugar and the Mongolian butter *shar-tos*. According to the customs, the fattest sheep is sacrificed and the lower back and tail are boiled and placed at the centre of the table for the period of Tsagaan Sar. The New Year's Eve is called *bituun* – the last dinner of the old year. After the stars come out, incense sticks

Preparations for Tsagaan Sar, or the Lunar New Year, begin nearly a month ahead. The female members start preparing hundreds of meat dumplings and various milk products.

are lit and Mongolian tea is made. The first four bowls are sprinkled in the four directions and then the host takes a sip, followed by the guests. After the ceremony the lamb sacrum is cut and distributed, and thereafter, the dishes are served.

The following morning everyone rises before sunrise. They greet the sun and take the 'first steps' of the New Year. Then the greetings start – with the oldest being greeted first. The second oldest person in the family carries a *khadag* on both palms, with a silver bowl filled with milk placed on the right palm, which is offered to the oldest member of the family. The younger member, with palms facing upward, grasp the elder one's elbow, whose palms face down and arms are above the younger one's. Throughout the day, and the next two days as well, family members, friends and relatives visit each other – greeting them, exchanging gifts, eating dishes made for the occasion, and drinking vodka and *kumis*. Elders are offered

Enjoying their Mongolian tea!

*khadag*s, while others are gifted snuff bottles as per ancient Mongolian tradition. On the first evening of the New Year, Mongolians also play traditional games, play musical instruments, and sing. The whole festivity lasts for a minimum of three days, though the greetings continue for almost two weeks.

NAADAM

The national sports festival is called Naadam. From ancient times, wrestling, archery and horse racing have been very popular among Mongolians. These are also called the 'three manly sports'. Hitherto, competitions in these were held during religious festivals. Since 1922, Naadam contests are held coinciding with the anniversary of the People's Revolution – on 11-13 July. The main opening ceremony of the festival is held at Naadam Stadium in

Women archers compete at the annual Naadam festival. Women shoot on a range of 60 metres.

Ulaanbaatar, on 11 July. This tradition was instituted by D. Sukhbaatar, the hero of the revolution. The opening ceremony consists of a military parade, cultural events, and a float depicting Mongolia's economic progress. Soon after, wrestling and archery contests start at the stadium, while the horse-racing competition is held about 30 kilometres outside the capital. Similar events are held in all the provincial capitals as well.

Wrestling is considered to be the most important and popular of all sports in Mongolia. Mongolian wrestling is distinctly different – with no weight or age categories. The wrestlers wear heavy boots, tight-fitting loincloth, and a tiny jacket. They go out on the field in a flurry of movement, leaping and flapping their arms like an eagle. The aim of the wrestler is to knock the opponent off balance and throw him down, making him touch the ground with his elbow or knee. The loser walks under the raised arm of the winner as a sign of respect. This is the most civilised and the least violent form of wrestling one might perhaps see. Considering the popularity of the sport, a national decree has been issued to regulate the titles of winners. At Naadam, nine rounds are held. A wrestler who wins in five rounds is awarded the title Republican Falcon, and the one who wins seven rounds earns the title of Elephant. The wrestler who wins the competition by winning all the nine rounds is called Lion, and the one

*Left: **Top:** A tableau at a local Naadam festival.*
***Below:** There is a distinct hierarchy of winners in Mongolian wrestling.*

Archery is an extension of the military training practised for centuries by Mongolian clans. Archers use a composite bow made of layered horn, bark and wood.

99

who wins for two consecutive years is a Giant. A three-time champion at Naadam is honoured as Invincible.

Horse racing is another essential sport of Naadam. There, the horses are generally divided in the age groups of two, three, four, five, over five, and stallion. Riders are usually in the age groups of five to twelve years. Adults used to take part earlier, but to reduce the weight on the horse and to increase its speed, now children are specially trained for these races. The distance varies according to the category of horse – it can be between 15 and 40 kilometres. The winners are honoured, but there are no titles as in the case of wrestling. The owners of the winning horses enjoy a special social status.

The third element of the Naadam sports is archery. Chinggis Khan and his warriors were able to win several wars because of their expertise in the art of archery. During the Naadam competition, Mongols use a compound bow built up of horn, sinew, bark and wood. Men shoot a distance of 75 metres, while women shoot on a range of 60 metres. The winners are honoured at the end of the competition. According to historical records, the art of archery was much more developed at the time of Chinggis Khan – when archers used to shoot multiple arrows from moving objects up to a distance of one kilometre with great accuracy.

THE TSAATANS

The Tsaatan people, better known as the 'reindeer people', are quite different compared to the other nomadic tribes of Mongolia. The word 'tsaatan' comes from the Mongolian *tsaa*, which translates into 'reindeer'. The Tsaatans trace their origin to a Tuvan ethnic group in the Tuva republic of Russia. These people, not more than a thousand in total, constitute the smallest ethnic group of Mongolia and their number is gradually decreasing.

In the main, the Tsaatans can be found in the cold mountainous area of Huvsgul aimag spreading over several thousand kilometres. They practise Shamanism and their existence primarily revolves around the domesticated reindeers. They do not live in the traditional *ger*, but prefer a conical tent made of reindeer skin. They sleep on the ground and use reindeer skin to cover the floor. Reindeer milk and meat make up their chief diet, while the skin is used for clothing. The people also occasionally consume meat of other animals.

Reindeers also provide the Tsaatans their means of transport. They are a truly nomadic people and move every few weeks with their reindeers from one mountain to another.

A young Tsaatan boy rides a frisky calf. The 'reindeer people' regularly move from one place to another in search of food for their flock.

Since reindeers like a special variety of grass and moss, the people move from place to place in search of food for their flock. Their encampment is called *ail*. The Tsaatans prefer the cold mountainous region and avoid travelling to the steppe grassland. Occasionally, a few families go down to Huvsgul Lake during the summer months for short durations.

So far, the Mongolian government's efforts to persuade the Tsaatans to send their children to schools have not yielded any positive results. Although their living conditions are extremely harsh and primitive even by nomadic standards, they prefer to follow their ancestral traditions. It is a remarkable feat, indeed, that they have remained immune to change even in this era of globalisation and modernity. Ancient traditions and customs continue to be at the heart of their lifestyle and thought process.

Wood is the only fuel the Tsaatans use in their traditional stove. Reindeer milk and meat chiefly constitute their diet, while the skin is used for clothing.

Religion

Religion is often viewed as humanity's attempt to discover the unknown, the unexplained, or the mysterious, or to overcome the natural disasters that befall. It was natural that the Mongolian nomads worshipped the forces of nature to overcome calamities like heavy snow, strong winds, thunder, lightning, heavy rains, and draught, or even illness. The sun, the moon, the stars, the earth, the sky, the mountains, the lakes, and the rivers were all regarded as having a profound impact on their daily lives and, in fact, on their very existence. Thus, 'nature worshipping' – the precursor to Shamanism – came to be the earliest religion among Mongolians.

Left: Lamas chant, ring bells, blow horns, and beat drums during prayers at Gandan Monastery, Mongolia.

Young novices at Gandan Monastery.

☞ SHAMANISM

The *tengeri* (sky or heaven), with its infinite expanse and mysterious changes, became the most important object of worship. People revered the *tengeri* as a supreme universe containing 99 heavens – 55 of these were considered good for mankind and the rest 44 were feared as furious and arrogant. The earth was regarded as 'mother'. The North Star, or Altan Khadaas, with six other stars (seven old men) also acquired a special status among the nomadic people. The Altan Khadaas also served as navigational guide on the vast Gobi desert, devoid as it was of any landmarks. Other natural forces – the sun, the moon, the stars, the mountains, the rivers, and fire – all acquired sacred meaning over time. In order to overcome a natural calamity or an illness, the forces of nature were invoked with special prayers.

In time, several practices evolved – some survive till date. Even today, the Mongolian president takes his official oath in the name of the 'blue sky'. In ancient times the official decrees used to be issued in the name of 'heaven and earth'. The *Secret History of the Mongols* was commissioned to be written on white paper with blue cover. The festivities of Tsagaan Saar begin with prayers to the sun. Mongols believe that natural phenomena such as mountains, lakes and rivers are seats of local deities. Hence, even today, several mountains, lakes and rivers are worshipped in Mongolia. The *ovoo* is always placed on top of a mountain or a hill. Fire has been an object of worship because of its light, warmth and cooking properties. There is a strong belief in the cleansing quality of fire. In ancient times, visitors of the khan were required to pass between two large fires as a purification ritual before an audience at the court. Worship of fire and use of fire for ritualistic practices is still common in Mongolia.

The veneration of ancestors is another Shamanist practice. There is a common belief that an ancestral spirit may either bless or curse a family depending upon the family's attitude and action. Chinggis Khan is even today regarded as the protector of the Mongol state. Animal sacrifice, particularly to please ancestors or local deities, has also been common. It was quite common to invoke the protective power of local deities before big battles. Sprinkling of mare's milk before commencement of rituals is still common among nomads. Since the horse is their supreme animal, certain products of the animal are considered to be blessed. Fortune telling from the shoulder bone of a sheep is a tradition that still survives.

In course of time, the nomadic practices evolved into poetic chants, rituals and mystical powers. It was believed that a true Shaman was able to put himself in trance and communicate with gods or spirits – and by so doing, the Shaman was able to exorcise evil spirits to cure sicknesses or overcome natural disasters. Thus, Shamans were considered to be mediators between the people and the blue sky, their supreme God. Some Shamans were thought to possess powers to call for rain, cause thunder, get rivers to stop or to flow in the opposite direction, and ward off evil spirit. They were also believed to be possessed of powers to predict the future with accuracy. Thus, the Shamans have played a prominent role in the courts of Mongol rulers, from the Huns right up to the time of the Kidans. There were several Shamanist temples during the Hun dynasty. Modun Khan of that dynasty was respected as the 'son of the blue sky'. Kokechu and Dev Tenger, well-known Shamans during the reign of Chinggis Khan, enjoyed considerable powers in the court. Munkh Khan had to issue a decree that anyone placing a curse on another person would be sentenced to death.

Unlike the adherents of many other religions, the Shamans were not fanatics. They accepted the deities and rituals of other religions and interpreted those as manifestations of Shamanism. Thus, religious freedom and tolerance were an accepted practice among

Mountain ovoo – a shamanistic collection of stones, wood and other offerings to the gods, usually located in high places.

This woman, a renowned shaman of Tsaatan, could tell nomads when they should move to greener pastures for their reindeer herds.

Mongol khans. It is believed that Christian churches, Buddhist monasteries, Muslim mosques and other places of worship coexisted in Karakorum. People were free to celebrate the festivals of different faiths and religions. Religious tolerance helped the khans to rule the vast empire. Undoubtedly, a great positive contribution of the Mongols was harmonious existence of various religions – the roots of which rest in Shamanism.

With the spread of Buddhism, Shamanism as a religion of the masses declined. From the 17th century onwards, Shamanism practically became extinct. However, several Shamanist practices became an integral part of Buddhism.

✆ BUDDHISM

There is evidence that Buddhism first appeared in Mongolia in the 3rd century BC, during the Hun period. According to historical records, a three-metre tall golden Buddha statue existed during this period, and it is thought to have been a widely accepted object of sacrifices. At the time of

Right: Erdene Zuu monastery in Mongolia.

Buddhist temple in Ulaanbaatar.

Tsong Khapa rock statue.

the Nirun state (Juan-juan Khanate, AD 402-555), Buddhism was widely accepted. Some historians state that it was even declared the state religion during this period, though the claim is disputed. A few historical writings indicate that Lama Dharmpria was appointed a religious teacher in AD 420.

Buddhism and Shamanism coexisted during the Turkic and Uighur periods. The Kidans established the first Buddhist monastery in AD 902. After founding of the unified Mongol Empire, Chinggis Khan invited several Buddhist lamas from Tibet and India. According to an old Mongolian chronicle, when Chinggis Khan was on his way to India (Hindusun) chasing Jalal-ad-Din (son of Khorezm ruler Muhammad), he saw a Bodhi deer (Bodhi *gorosun*) on the banks of Sindhu River (Sindu-Murun). The deer bowed before the Mongol king. Touched by the gesture, Chinggis Khan was convinced that India was a sacred land that could not be conquered. He not only retraced his steps, but also brought with him two Buddhist monks to Karakorum. Based on this old legend, Mongolians even today describe India as 'spiritual neighbour' or 'brother of dharma'.

According to the biography of Tieh-Ko (Tege), a Buddhist devotee from Kashmir, Namo, was received at the court of Ogodei Khan with great respect. He was subsequently given the title of teacher, with the authority to supervise all Buddhist affairs. Ogodei Khan's son Koton, after his campaign against Tibet, had the Tibetan Buddhist master Saskya Pandita brought to his court. Saskya was accompanied by his nephew Phags-pa, who lived in the Mongol court for several years and became a close friend of Kubilai Khan. Buddhism was proclaimed the state religion of Kubilai Khan's Yuan dynasty. Phags-pa was given the title 'Teacher of the Realm' and, later, also conferred with the status of 'Imperial Tutor'. Kubilai Khan granted several privileges to Buddhist lamas from time to time, and used to consult them for an auspicious time and place before the commencement of any important ceremony or battle. Kubilai Khan also established a separate office, Hsuan Chong Yuan, with jurisdiction over all religious affairs of the realm. The head of the organisation worked under the direction of the Imperial Tutor. After the disintegration of the Mongol Empire in 1368, Buddhism also lost its predominance among the Mongol tribes, though it remained a popular religion.

Dayan Khan, who acceded to the Mongolian throne in 1470, made feeble attempts to revive Buddhism. His grandson Altan Khan, who succeeded in reuniting the feudal lords and concluded a peace treaty with Ming China in 1570, spearheaded the revival of Buddhism in a big way. In 1578 Altan Khan invited Sonam Gyatso, the head of the dominant Yellow Sect of Tibetan Buddhism, to visit Mongolia. On the occasion, Altan Khan bestowed on him the title Dalai – meaning 'as immense as the ocean.' Later on, Sonam Gyatso came to be known as the third Dalai Lama and his predecessors were posthumously designated as the first and second Dalai Lamas. Thus, the title of Dalai Lama is said to have originated in Mongolia.

Lamaism took strong roots in Mongolia, replacing the earlier form of Buddhism. In 1586 the famous Erdene Zuu Monastery in Karakorum was established.

Mongolians gather during a Buddhist procession.

Lamaism was well suited to Mongolian conditions for several reasons. First, it was able to assimilate Shamanist practices. Its rituals, ceremonies, gods and goddesses, tantric and mystical elements, and religious arts were similar to the Shamanist rituals in Mongolia. As an example of the extent of assimilation, the *ovoo* soon became a symbol of Buddhism. Secondly, the Mongol aristocracy favoured Lamaism because they wanted their status to be reinforced by religious heads, or the lamas. Thirdly, the Ming rulers also found it convenient to use Lamaism as an instrument for pacification of the warlike and fierce Mongolian tribes. Thus, Lamaism started spreading rapidly among both the feudal lords as also among the masses in Mongolia.

In the 17th century, Ligden Khan (1604-34) and Undur Gegeen Zanabazar (1635-1723) played leading roles in the consolidation of Buddhism in Mongolia. Ligden Khan ordered the translation and printing of two monumental religious and literary works, *Kanjur* and *Tanjur*. *Kanjur* is primarily a collection of Buddhist teachings by renowned sages such as Nagarjuna, Asanga, Vasubandu, Dignage, Dharmakirti and Dharmottara. It has 109 volumes containing 1,162 chapters. There are several editions of *Kanjur* – one of them was written with nine

114

precious stones, and another one in gold. While some works were taken away by the Manchu rulers to Inner Mongolia, most of them are presently in the custody of the State Library in Ulaanbaatar. A project to digitalise these precious manuscripts is presently underway.

The 224-volume *Tanjur* is a collection of learned writings in subjects like philosophy, mathematics, literature, medicine and political thoughts, by well-known Indian scholars such as Valmiki, Panini, Patanjali, Kalidas, Dandin, Ratnakara, Asvakosa, Chanakya and Charak. All these writings from Sanskrit, Tibetan and Pali were translated into Mongolian by several Mongolian scholars over a period of about two centuries. Initially, a group of 35 scholars was formed under the guidance of Gungaa Odser.

From the second half of the 16th century until the beginning of the 20th, Buddhism flourished in Mongolia. At the end of the 19th century, there were more than one thousand Buddhist monasteries and prayer places all over Mongolia, with more than 100,000 lamas. The religious school of Gandan Monastery, established in 1739, produced several highly educated and learned lamas. Literary writings and religious art were at their peak. Hundreds of literary, philosophical and scientific writings from India and Tibet were translated and made available to the common people. In this way, Buddhism helped considerably in the development of Mongolian culture and civilisation. During this period, nearly every aspect of life and culture in Mongolia had a profound imprint of Buddhism.

Soon after the People's Revolution in 1921, repressive measures were taken against all religious activities, particularly Buddhism. During 1929-32, nearly 300 monasteries were closed and thousands of lamas were forced to work outside. Later, though, some of them were allowed to reopen. According to official statistics, in 1936 there were 767 monasteries and over 100,000 lamas in Mongolia. Buddhist institutions in Mongolia suffered a serious blow, once more, during Stalin's crackdown on religious institutions in 1937-38. Almost all the

Lamas pray on raised platforms in front of Gandan Monastery.

Facing page: *A wooden chorten constructed to commemorate the dead.*

monasteries were destroyed – some were burnt, while others were bombed. Thousands of lamas were killed and the rest were forced to quit religious life. Several thousand books, religious paintings and artworks were destroyed. The largest copper statue of the Buddha was removed from Gandan Monastery and reportedly used for making bullets.

For the next 40 years or so, Mongolians worshipped in the privacy of their homes. With the democratic revolution in Mongolia in 1990, religious freedom was restored. Since 1990 some monasteries have been repaired and restored. At present, there are about 200 monasteries and places of worship in Mongolia. Gandan Monastery in Ulaanbaatar, Erdene Zuu in Karakorum, and Amarbayalsaglant Monastery near Darkhan are among the most prominent.

In the post-1990 period, Christian missionaries have also become very active. It is estimated that about 200 Christian NGOs (non-government organisations) are operating in various parts of the country. On the whole, about 90 per cent Mongolians believe in Buddhism, about 5 per cent in Islam, and the rest in other religions. Followers of Islam are primarily confined to the western province of Bayan-Ulgii. They are primarily of Kazakh origin.

Colourful masks of the sacred tsam *dance. The masks symbolise the demon (*dogshin*) and the peaceful (*amirlangui*) Buddhist deities.*

☙ TSAM DANCE

The *tsam*, or mask, dance is one of the most significant religious rituals in Mongolia. The dance was first introduced into Mongolia in the 16th century, and was brought from Tibet. In Mongolia, the *tsam* was further enriched with the tantric elements of Shamanism. As a result,

the Mongolian masks, costumes and movements are somewhat different from those in Tibet, India and Bhutan. The costumes are more colourful, while the masks are exceptionally large and highly artistic, and adorned with gold, silver and precious stones. The *tsam* masks symbolise the 'demon' (*dogshin*) and the 'peaceful' (*amirlangui*) Buddhist deities. It is believed that the *tsam* enacts rituals and scenes from the lives of heaven-dwellers and heroes. This ritual is performed once a year, normally in July, across monasteries in Mongolia to exorcise evil. The movements and gestures of the actors are symbolic of the triumph of good over evil, of enlightenment over darkness, and of life over death, as contained in the Sanskrit sloka – *asto ma satgamoy, tamso ma jyotirgamoy, mrityor ma amritamgamoy. Tsam* dances are not only a spectacle of the mesmerising beauty of colour, motion and sound, but are also divine offerings for the destruction of evil. While performing the *tsam*, dancers pray and softly chant Buddhist mantras. Given the elaborate nature of this religious ritual, it requires months of preparation. *Tsam* dancers are required to pray, meditate and observe dietary restrictions for at least a month in advance. The *tsam* festival at Amarbayalsaglant Monastery near Darkhan is considered to be the most fascinating of all.

✆ RELIGIOUS LITERATURE

Despite the indiscriminate destruction of precious religious literature during the Manchu and Stalin eras, Mongolia remains a treasure-house of Buddhist literature. The State Public Library alone houses over two million manuscripts. These include a book on tree bark written about 2,500 years ago. Gandan Monastery and Erdene Zuu as well as several private museums and libraries are in possession of several precious manuscripts. The State Public Library also has a copy of an 11th-century manuscript, *Jadamba*, written in gold. The library's Tibetan section contains works of ancient scholars, thinkers and writers. The *Kanjur* and the *Tanjur* are a treasure for scholars and researchers.

Prayer flags featuring Buddhist mantras.

ZANABAZAR

Undur Gegeen Zanabazar was born in 1635 in the present-day Uvurkhangai province of Mongolia, in the family of Tusheet Khan Gombodorj, one of the three major rulers of that time and a descendant of Chinggis Khan. Evidently, Zanabazar was a genius from his childhood. There are several stories describing his unusual behaviour and extraordinary talents. To illustrate, at the age of three he was able to recite Buddhist sutras and make replicas of Buddhist temples without any instructions or teachings. At the same age, according to another legend, Zanabazar was able to paint the city of Lhasa and Potala Palace without ever seeing it. When he was just five years old, the fifth Dalai Lama identified Zanabazar and bestowed on him the title of Mongolia's first Bogd Khan (religious king).

Zanabazar composed sacred music, perfected the art of bronze casting and refined the techniques of thangka painting, created a new design for monastic robes, and invented the Soyombo script.

At the age of 16, Zanabazar went to Tibet to study religion and philosophy, and returned after four years. He also brought several Tibetan monks and savants with him to Mongolia. In Tibet he learnt the art of bronze casting and over time became the greatest sculptor of Mongolia. After his return, he went on to become the most important religious and state figure of his time. He was a painter, sculptor, poet, writer, linguist, architect, and philosopher. In 1686 he invented a new alphabet called Soyombo. Although the alphabet did not become popular for a variety of reasons, the first letter of the alphabet became a symbol of Mongolia's independence and sovereignty, and was subsequently adopted as the state symbol and continues to remain so till date.

The word Soyombo originates in the Sanskrit word svayambhu, meaning 'self-existing' or 'self-sustaining'. A large number of bronze and copper statues sculpted by Zanabazar form part of the precious collection at the Zanabazar and Chojin Lama museums as well as at the Erdene Zuu monastery. The 21 statues of the goddess Tara and the five poses of the Buddha are regarded as some of his best sculptures. Zanabazar's Vajradara, presently in Gandantegchinlen Monastery in Ulaanbaatar, personifies all the tantric Buddhas in meditation. Zanabazar's sculptures are based on detailed geometric proportions of the human body as propounded by the Dashatala proportion of Indian art. Lotus pedestals, meditation and mudras, or symbolic gestures of hands and fingers, characterise most sculptures of Zanabazar. He founded the Mongolian classical religious school of art, which exists till date. The Fine Arts Museum in Ulaanbaatar has been named after him. Mongolian historians consider him as the Michelangelo of the Central Asia.

A few historians have criticised Zanabazar's close association with the Manchu rulers. However, given the realities of that time, perhaps he had no option but to accept their support. He was largely motivated by the desire to avoid any conflict with powerful Manchu China and imperial Russia. Moreover, Zanabazar helped in preserving Mongolia's independence by resisting the merger of Mongolia with Manchu territory. After his death in Beijing in 1723, his body was entombed in a stupa in Amarbayasaglant Monastery near present-day Darkhan city.

At the age of three Zanabazar was able to recite Buddhist sutras and make replicas of Buddhist temples without any instructions or teachings.

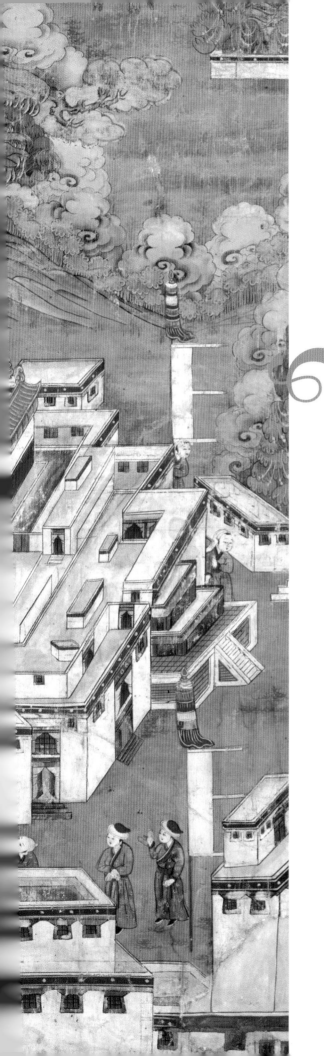

ART AND CULTURE

Mongolia has a rich and unique cultural tradition. The landscape, the nomadic way of life, and the religious traditions have greatly influenced the evolution of the country's cultural life. The clear blue sky, the star-studded nights, the snow-covered mountains, the crystal-clear blue lakes, the icy winds, the galloping horses, the milking of animals, the combing of wool and cashmere, and the long and lonely tracks, have all found an echo in Mongolian music, dances and paintings, in one way or another.

Paintings on religious themes dominated after the arrival of Tibetan Buddhism in Mongolia in the 16th and 17th centuries.

☙ MUSICAL TRADITIONS

Mongolia has a large variety of songs and musical instruments to suit any occasion. Among the signature Mongolian forms are the *khoomii*, or throat-singing; the *urtyn duu*, or long song; the epic songs; and the *morin khuur*, or horse-headed string instrument. There are songs for national festivals, wedding ceremonies, birthdays, wrestling competitions, breeding of animals, cashmere combing, making of felt, erecting of *ger*, and also the changing seasons.

Khoomii

The *khoomii* is a traditional form of singing wherein two or more sounds are produced simultaneously by manipulating the lungs and the vocal cord. These sounds are normally produced only by men, and require rigorous training of lungs, vocal cords and breathing techniques. It is more of a musical art, and not exactly a singing one, as one's throat is used as an instrument of music. Depending on the way the air is exhaled, there are several types of *khoomii* – *hooloin*, or guttural; *hamryn*, or nasal; *bagalzuuryn*, or laryngeal; and *harhiraa*, where the lower tone is kept as the main sound. The Hovd aimag in the western part of Mongolia is well known for producing several accomplished *khoomii* singers. The aimag has a long tradition of *khoomii*.

Urtyn Duu

Long songs are another form of vocal singing. It is one of the most ancient arts of Mongolia, influenced primarily by the vastness of nature and the long journeys in solitude. This type of singing also involves complicated and drawn-out vocal sounds involving the manipulation of breathing and vocal cords. Long songs can be sung by either a man or a woman, but they are always in solo. The singer is required to mix a wide range of tones and voices, and produce one single harmonious sound as long as possible while modulating the vowels. Long songs are often melancholic, recalling solitude or broken hearts. They also describe the beauty of nature. Nomads often sing such songs on horseback while traversing long routes.

Morin Khuur

The *morin khuur* is the most ancient, and also the most popular, string instrument in Mongolia. The Mongolian *mor* means 'horse' and *khuur* means 'sound' or 'melody'. The hair of a horse's tail is used to make the two strings of the instrument, while the head – similar to a horse's head – is carved out of wood. Since the horse is the most important animal in the life of a nomad, the instrument has been designed to honour the same. According to historians, the *morin khuur* was first invented in the 2nd century BC, during the Hun period. Initially, the upper end of the instrument was carved in the shape of Garuda, and only afterwards was it replaced by the horse head. According to a legend, a nomad named Khokhoo Namjil once had a horse that had two wings and could fly – much like it is narrated in *The Arabian Nights*. One day a jealous neighbour cut its wings and the horse died. Khokhoo Namjil, overtaken by grief, decided to make a musical instrument in honour and memory of his horse. It was then called the *morin khuur*.

The head of the morin khuur *resembles a horse's head. Here, a couple of musicians playing on the strings outdoors.*

The instrument is used to play a wide variety of musical pieces describing nature and animals. The sounds of galloping horses, gently flowing rivers, sandstorm in the Gobi, shifting sand dunes, and herd hooves are commonly played. The instrument is an essential accompaniment for Mongolian singing and dancing. In 2002, the *morin khuur* was declared as the national musical instrument of Mongolia by a presidential decree, and in 2004 it was included in UNESCO's list of World Heritage of Art and Cultural Objects.

Epic Songs

The epics and legends are part of Mongolia's oral traditions. Epic songs are a combination of music, song, poetry and drama, and are used to pass on traditional wisdom, folklore and historical narratives to the younger generation. This tradition is especially popular among the ethnic groups Dorvod, Bayat, Uriankhai and Torguud. Epic singing is considered sacred and, therefore, the musical instrument used for the singing is decorated with a *khadag* and the performance begins with a poetic praise, *magtaal*, dedicated to the Altai. Shamanist stories form an integral part of the epic. Two of the most popular epics are the *Geser* and the *Jangar*. It is believed that some epics have magical power and can help people to overcome poverty and illness, and even help a woman to bear a child. Most of the epic singing takes place in the long winter nights and continues till sunrise.

Other Musical Instruments

In addition to the *morin khuur*, there are several other traditional instruments played in Mongolia. These are: *yatga* – a horizontal string instrument; *shudorga* – a string instrument

similar to the sitar from India; *tumurkhuur* – a bamboo leaf resonance-based instrument; *limbe* – a flute-like instrument; *buree* – a trumpet; and *tsan khengereg* – an instrument similar to a drum. Of these, the *yatga*, *limbe* and *tsan khengereg* are still widely used.

🏇 DANCES

Mongolia has a strong tradition of folk dances. This tradition was particularly encouraged to cope with the harsh climatic conditions and the solitude often experienced amid the vast stretches of land. According to the *Secret History of the Mongols*, the people were apt at feasting, rejoicing and dancing.

Elaborate costumes, silver and gold jewellery, and a variety of headgears are used by the Mongolian folk dancers. Gestures of hands, chest, eyes and head are significant elements. Shamanist practices and nature worshipping form the core of Mongolian folk traditions. The movements of folk dancers often portray birds, animals, martial arts and Shamanist tantric practices. The dancers often dance with silver bowls, filled with drinks, positioned on their heads and palms in a delicate act of balancing while dancing. These are also known as cup dances. This tradition is particularly strong in the western aimags. Usually, competitions in these dances are held on festive occasions or during wedding ceremonies. Highly skilled dancers can perform dances with cups on their heads, palms and knees, without spilling a drop. The *bielgee* is a dance with the upper parts of the body, and is particularly popular in western Mongolia. This is primarily a solo dance performed in restricted space, with expressive movements of head, chest, hands, shoulders and eyes.

Different ethnic groups have their own variety of costumes and dance forms. Often, folk

Mongolian dancers dressed in traditional costumes at the Mongolian National Theatre in Ulaanbaatar.

Following pages 130-131: *A Mongolian man and woman perform a traditional folk dance on stage.*

dancers are accompanied by a *morin khuur* player. Since the beginning of the 20th century, the tradition of folk dances has suffered considerably – partly due to the popularity of ballet and Western classical dances introduced by the Soviet Union, and partly due to the infiltration of pop and disco music in the cities.

✿ CONTORTION

Contortion is a form of acrobatic display involving dramatic flexing and bending of the human body. This unusual performing art has a long and deep-rooted tradition in Mongolia. Mongolian contortion is usually performed by young girls in the age group of 6–14. The performance is either solo or in groups of four or five. Mongolian skills in this art are extremely versatile, with performers able to stretch themselves like rubber and appearing to be quite boneless and weightless. Mongolian contortionists can perform intricate gymnastics, gravity-defying postures and aerial spinning, among other things. They can also accomplish such delicate balancing as putting the whole body on two teeth or chin, and then rotating the body, legs and hands. Moreover, they do these acts with so much ease that spectators are left spellbound. Several Mongolian contortionists find their names among the best in the world. These include Norov Sambuu, Undermaa, Tumendelger and Mira. The Mongolian State Circus School offers comprehensive training courses for budding contortionists.

Female contortion artists executing their intricate movements.

An ancient Mongolian anthropomorphic statue.

Below: Detail of sculpture on roof of a monastery.

Facing page: A statue of the goddess Tara sculpted by Zanabazar.

ART, CRAFT AND SCULPTURES

Mongolia has an ancient tradition of art and craft, which include artefacts of iron and bronze, wood carvings, stone carvings, sculpture, ornamental appliqué on leather, embroidery on silk and felt, silver artefacts, and jewellery made of gold, silver and semi-precious stones. Long knives, saddles, artistic silver bowls, carved snuffboxes, and decorated copper utensils have been in use for centuries. Relics found at the Hunnu tomb in Noyon Uul date back to the 3rd century BC. These consist of jewellery, pottery, felt carpet and other artwork. The tradition and skills of old masters have been transmitted through generations by means of family and tribal folklore. The craftsmanship and designs of women's jewellery vary from tribe to tribe. Women's headdresses and hair jewellery are most complex and striking. During the Uighur Empire, Mongolian art and craft was fairly well-developed. Several stone carvings and ceramic vases from the 8th and 9th centuries have been found in the Orkhon River basin. Archaeologists have found several cast-iron objects going back to the 12th century. Scientists believe that metal processing had been fairly well-developed in Mongolia in ancient times, partly dictated by the needs of the nomads and partly by their war machine. The furniture in the *ger* is a characteristic example of wooden carvings. Deer carvings in rock and deer stones

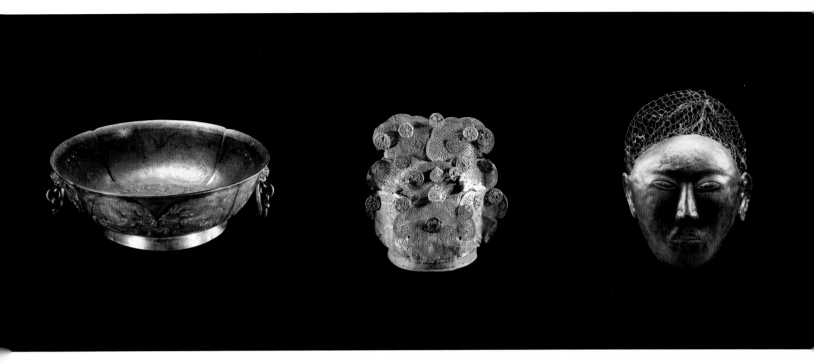

were quite common in ancient times. Over 550 deer stones have been found all over Mongolia. For centuries deer has been a sacred animal in Mongolia, and Mongolians believe that it can carry the spirit of the dead to the next life.

Buddhist rituals have also left a strong imprint on Mongolian artistic traditions. Cast images of the Buddha, masks for *tsam* dances, *thangka*s and metal objects used in monasteries, were particularly influenced by Buddhist traditions. Embroidery works on silk and felt also bear a distinct influence of Buddhism. Some of these artistic traditions were also influenced by Shamanistic practices and nature worshipping. In the 16th and 17th centuries, Zanabazar and his followers produced remarkable masterpieces in bronze which are comparable to the best artworks anywhere in the world. In order to produce perfect body proportions, they used elaborate methods of geometry. The 21 Taras created by Zanabazar are examples of the high artistic tradition of the time.

The religious school of Gandan produced several great artists who created beautiful *thangka*s, silk appliqué and bronze sculptures. A similar school was set up at Amarbayasaglant Monastery in 1723. During this period, Mongolian masters developed the sophisticated art of writing with gold, silver and semi-precious stones.

✎ Paintings

The rock and cave paintings found in the Dundgobi, Uvurkhangai and Hovd aimags are a clear testimony to the ancient tradition of painting in Mongolia, dating to the Bronze Age. Rock paintings at the Khoit-Tsenkher cave in Hovd are the oldest paintings found so far. Archaeological finds from Uighur Empire also confirm the ancient tradition of this art in Mongolia. Some Mongolian paintings of this period preserved in Tokapi Museum in Istanbul

Left to right: *A silver platter; a crown ornament; a gold mask.*

Facing page: *A mask used in the* tsam *dance.*

primarily depict cattle-breeders, hunting scenes, wrestling and war scenes. The paintings of the 13th and 14th centuries mainly reflect the nomadic lifestyle and the beauty of the Mongolian landscape. Chinggis Khan's portrait drawn in 1278 under the instruction of his grandson Kubilai, is still preserved in Taipei.

Paintings on religious themes dominated after the arrival of Tibetan Buddhism in the 16th and 17th centuries. During this period two separate schools emerged – one based on religious themes and another based on nature and the daily life of a nomad. *Thangka*s and paintings based on *Kalachakra* (a Buddhist religious philosophy and practice) and *Jataka* (stories based on the Buddha's life) are typical examples of religious paintings. Mongolian religious paintings are refined and have perfect geometric proportions based on the artistic teachings of Chitralakshana from ancient India. B. Sharav (1839–1939) produced several masterpieces on the theme of the nomadic life. An example is his work *One Day in Mongolia*. Since the early 20th century, Mongolia has also produced several master painters in modern art. Prominent names include O. Tsevegjav, U. Yadamsuren, N. Chultem, G. Odon, L. Gavaa, A. Sengetsokhio, B. Avarzed and T. Dorjpalam. Most of them are well known in art circles all over the world.

Facing page:
Creative expression on the door of a ger.

Boulder painted with deity.

138

MUSEUMS

The National Museum of Mongolian History, founded in 1924, was the first museum in Mongolia. It houses over 40,000 archaeological, historical and ethnographic objects.

These include some rare objects from the period between 3rd century BC and 1st century BC, coinciding with the Hun period. The Museum of Natural History, established in 1966, houses objects pertaining to Mongolia's natural history, geology, botany, zoology and palaeontology. The main attractions of this museum are the skeletons, fossils and eggs of giant dinosaurs that roamed the Gobi Desert millions of years ago. The largest dinosaur skeleton is 12 metres long and 5 metres tall. The Zanabazar Museum of Fine Arts was established in 1966. It features artworks from ancient times until the early 20th century. Exhibits include prehistoric rock carvings, several masterpieces of Zanabazar and B. Sharav, *tsam* masks and *thangka*s. The Bogd Khan Museum, which was originally the winter palace of the last Bogd Khan, houses palace objects and masterpieces of Buddhist art. The Mongolian National Modern Art Gallery, established in 1989, has a collection of modern paintings and traditional Mongolian fine art. The gallery houses more than 6,000 paintings, sculptures and appliqué. In addition, each of the aimag capitals in Mongolia boasts of a museum depicting the history, nature and culture of the particular aimag. Some of these museums house rare objects going back to the 1st century BC.

A close-up of the contents of the dinosaur egg nest discovery. The eggs, about 6 inches long, are estimated to be 1,000,000,000 years old.

Facing page: *Dinosaur skeleton in museum, Mongolia.*

Cashmere – a soft and warm natural fibre

Cashmere is one of the softest, warmest and most durable natural fibres. The more it is worn, the softer it becomes. Cashmere wool could be even eight times warmer than sheep wool. Due to these qualities, combined with its limited availability, cashmere is one of the most expensive natural fibres.

The word 'cashmere' originates in the fine wool derived from Kashmiri goats found in the Himalayas. Cashmere wool comes from the undercoat that grows on goats from mid-summer to winter to keep them warm in the winter. This is like a new layer of natural warm clothing. The long hair on goats called guard hair protects the cashmere underneath.

goats. The cashmere-producing goats in Mongolia are called Yama. Yield from Mongolian goats average 300-500 grams per goat. Eighty per cent of the cashmere produced has a micron of 16.5 with a length of 35-37 millimetres. In the 1940s the Soviets introduced an Angora crossbreeding stock called the Don Goat in the Gobi region, and crossbred them with the Mongolian goats. The resulting breed was called Gobi Gurvan Saikhan (GGS). However, the quality of fibre of the crossbred goats was poorer. Gray, brown and white are natural cashmere colours, but the fibre can be dyed to produce a range of other colours.

Cashmere fibres are collected each spring either by combing or by shearing the animal during the moulting period. The quality of cashmere wool is measured by its length and texture, and by the diameter of the fibre.

Harsh, dry and mountainous regions are particularly suitable for cashmere goats. Most of the world's cashmere production comes from China, Tibet, Mongolia and Kashmir in India. The climate and geography of Mongolia are particularly suited for such

With a cashmere goat population of around 12 million, Mongolia is the second largest producer of cashmere in the world – with a total annual production of about 3,000 tonnes of raw cashmere. The country accounts for about 25 per cent of total world production.

Cashmere processing industry in Mongolia is reasonably well developed. There are over 80 enterprises with local and foreign investments in the country. However, more

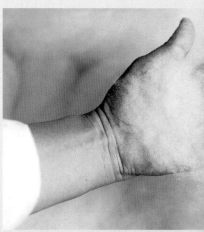

than 60 per cent of these are engaged in washing and scouring activities, while the rest are processing companies producing woven garments and other finished products. Gobi cashmere, Buyan and Goyo are the three largest enterprises producing a wide range of cashmere garments that are exported primarily to Europe, the United States and Japan. Cashmere products are the third largest export of the country after copper and gold. Raw cashmere constitutes 10 per cent, scoured cashmere 50 per cent, and woven cashmere 40 per cent of the total value of exports. Total production of woven cashmere is around 280 tonnes, or 1.5 million articles.

Cashmere fibres are collected either by combing or shearing the animal. The quality of cashmere wool is measured by its length and texture and by the diameter of the fibre.
Facing page: Yama, the cashmere-producing goats from Mongolia. Cashmere wool comes from the undercoat that grows on the goats.

PHOTO CREDITS

Mongolians in their traditional dress during the annual Naadam festival.